ICFA Continuing Education
Equity Research and Valuation Techniques

Proceedings of the AIMR seminar "Equity Research and Valuation Techniques"

December 9, 1997
Philadelphia, Pennsylvania

B. Kemp Dolliver, CFA
Alfred G. Jackson, CFA
Martin L. Leibowitz
Thomas A. Martin, Jr., CFA

Patrick O'Donnell
James A. Ohlson
Fred H. Speece, Jr., CFA, *Moderator*
Timothy J. Timura, CFA

Edited by Jan R. Squires, CFA

To obtain the *AIMR Publications Catalog,* contact:
AIMR, P.O. Box 3668, Charlottesville, Virginia 22903, U.S.A.
Phone 804-980-3668; Fax 804-980-9755; E-mail info@aimr.org
or
visit AIMR's World Wide Web site at **www.aimr.org**
to view the AIMR publications list.

ICFA Continuing Education is published monthly seven times a year in May, May, May, June, July, August, and September by the Association for Investment Management and Research, P.O. Box 3668, Charlottesville, Virginia 22903, U.S.A. This publication is designed to provide accurate and authoritative information with regard to the subject matter covered. It is sold with the understanding that the publisher is not engaged in rendering legal, accounting, or other professional services. If legal advice or other expert assistance is required, the services of a competent professional should be sought. Periodicals postage paid at the post office in Richmond, Virginia, and additional mailing offices.

Copies are mailed as a benefit of membership to CFA® charterholders. Subscriptions also are available at US$100 for one year. Address all circulation communications to ICFA Continuing Education, P.O. Box 3668, Charlottesville, Virginia 22903, U.S.A.; Phone 804-980-3668; Fax 804-980-9755. For change of address, send mailing label and new address six weeks in advance.

Postmaster: Send address changes to the Association for Investment Management and Research, P.O. Box 3668, Charlottesville, Virginia 22903.

ISBN 0-935015-21-3
Printed in the United States of America
May 1998

Editorial Staff

Maryann Dupes
Editor

Jaynee M. Dudley
Production Manager

Fiona D. Russell
Assistant Editor

Christine P. Martin
Production Coordinator

Lois A. Carrier
Diane B. Hamshar
Composition

Contents

Foreword

The Dow Jones Industrial Average broke not only the 7000 mark in 1997 but also the 8000 mark, and in April 1998, it broke 9000. This rapid growth of the U.S. equity market has left many investors wondering whether the market, and hence individual stocks, are overvalued. The only way to truly answer this question is to conduct research and value the securities. Of course, investors and analysts have been researching companies and valuing securities since the dawn of the profession, but the 1990s have seen the introduction of new methodologies and refinements of the old.

This emphasis on both the old and the new comes through clearly in this proceedings. The authors look at the tried-and-true valuation and research methodologies from a new perspective and review some of the new methodologies from a practical standpoint. They discuss using research from Wall Street analysts and from the Internet. They provide new insights into the traditional equity valuation methods, such as the price-to-earnings ratio, and they discuss cash flow analysis as a way of avoiding the problems inherent in earnings-based measures. The authors also present the advantages, and disadvantages, of using some of the new present value methodologies, such as economic value added and sales-driven franchise value. At the heart of all the discussions is the notion that analysts and investors must use not only their analytical but also their creative skills to determine whether a stock is priced appropriately.

This proceedings is based on AIMR's "Equity Research and Valuation Techniques" seminar held December 9, 1997. We are grateful to Fred H. Speece, Jr., CFA, Speece, Lewis & Thorson, for his work as both moderator of the seminar and author. We also wish to thank all the other authors for their valuable contributions and insights: B. Kemp Dolliver, CFA, Cowen & Company; Alfred G. Jackson, CFA, Credit Suisse First Boston; Martin L. Leibowitz, TIAA-CREF; Thomas A. Martin, Jr., CFA, INVESCO Capital Management Incorporated; Patrick O'Donnell, Putnam Investment Management; James A. Ohlson, Columbia University, Graduate School of Business; Timothy J. Timura, CFA, Pilgrim Baxter Value Investors, Inc.

Although researching and valuing securities is certainly far from a novel idea, the authors in this proceedings emphasize that it never goes out of style. Only through researching and valuing securities can investors answer the ultimate question of investing: Is this stock (or the market) fairly priced?

Katrina F. Sherrerd, CFA
Senior Vice President
Educational Products

Biographies

B. Kemp Dolliver, CFA, is a vice president at Cowen & Company, where he is responsible for research coverage in the acute care and behavioral health sectors of the health care industry. Previously, he held positions as senior portfolio manager and analyst at Trade Street Investment Associates and as a securities analyst at Aetna Life & Casualty. Mr. Dolliver received a B.S. from the McIntire School of Commerce, University of Virginia, and an M.B.A. from the Darden School, University of Virginia.

Alfred G. Jackson, CFA, is a managing director and global research director for equity products at Credit Suisse First Boston. He joined the firm as a vice president and food industry analyst and has also held the positions of director of equity research, national sales manager for U.S. equity products, global sales manager, and co-head of European equity. Prior to joining Credit Suisse First Boston, Mr. Jackson was a food industry analyst with Pershing & Company and Merrill Lynch & Company. He holds B.A. and M.B.A. degrees from Columbia University.

Martin L. Leibowitz is vice chairman and chief investment officer for TIAA–CREF, where he is responsible for the overall management of all TIAA–CREF investments. He joined the organization as executive vice president of CREF Investments. Previously, Mr. Leibowitz was at Salomon Brothers, Inc, where he served as a managing director, director of research for both fixed income and equities, and a member of the firm's executive committee. In 1995, Mr. Leibowitz received AIMR's Nicholas Molodovsky Award and also became the first inductee into the Fixed Income Analysts Society's Hall of Fame. Mr. Leibowitz holds B.A. and M.S. degrees from the University of Chicago and a Ph.D. in mathematics from the Courant Institute of New York University.

Thomas A. Martin, Jr., CFA, is an equity portfolio manager with INVESCO Capital Management Incorporated, an institutional money management firm. Previously the director of research at Hamilton, Allen & Associates, he has also held the position of equity securities analyst at Trusco Capital Management. Mr. Martin has taught a course called "Foundations of Investments" for those unfamiliar with the financial markets. He holds an A.B. in economics from Duke University.

Patrick O'Donnell is managing director and chief of global equity research at Putnam Investment Management, where he is a member of the management, executive, and capital markets committees. Prior to joining Putnam, he was principal of Exeter Research, and he was previously managing director in international equities research at Prudential Securities. Mr. O'Donnell has also held the positions of vice president at Furman Selz and at Donaldson, Lufkin & Jenrette. He received a B.A. from Harvard University and a Ph.D. from Princeton University.

James A. Ohlson is the George O. May Professor of Accounting at Columbia University, Graduate School of Business. Professor Ohlson's research has focused on accounting theory and the role of accounting data in equity valuation contexts. He has published extensively in the academic literature and has also lectured on equity valuation at universities and to professional audiences in the United States, Asia, Europe, and Australia. Professor Ohlson received M.B.A. and Ph.D. degrees from the University of California at Berkeley.

Fred H. Speece, Jr., CFA, is a founder of the investment management firm of Speece, Lewis & Thorson. He is on the Board of Governors of AIMR, chair of the Board of Trustees of the Institute of Chartered Financial Analysts, a trustee of the Research Foundation of the Institute of Chartered Financial Analysts, and chair of the Board of Regents of the Financial Analysts Seminar. He has been an adjunct faculty member in the Graduate School of Business at the University of St. Thomas and the University of Minnesota. He holds a B.B.A. from Ohio University and an M.B.A. from Western Michigan University.

Timothy J. Timura, CFA, is a portfolio manager at Pilgrim Baxter Value Investors, formerly Newbold's Asset Management, where he is responsible for large-capitalization value portfolio management. Mr. Timura previously served as senior manager in equities for the State Teachers Retirement System of Ohio and as an assistant vice president at Federated Investors. He has also taught graduate and undergraduate finance courses at Ohio State University. Mr. Timura received a B.A. from Dickinson College and an M.B.A. in finance from the University of Wisconsin at Madison.

Equity Research and Valuation Techniques: An Overview

Jan R. Squires, CFA
Professor of Finance
Southwest Missouri State University

No activity in the investment profession is practiced by more participants with more fervor than equity analysis and valuation. The allure of stocks, and the enthusiasm of stock investors, is as old as the profession itself; in fact, it predates the time when this collection of practices could even be called a profession. The techniques and methods for valuing equity instruments—from earnings to cash flows, from simple multiples to incredibly complex models, from the dividend discount model to the capital asset pricing model and beyond—have an equally rich past and have become part of the everyday investment landscape. Given such a setting, replete with a long history, legions of participants, and a seemingly inexhaustible supply of tools, can anything new be said about equity valuation? Can equity investors still expect new insights, new approaches, and new understandings to appear?

The answer is a resounding yes. The investment environment at the end of this century requires that equity analysts and investors face unparalleled challenges—working globally, dealing with a blizzard of information, satisfying increasingly demanding clients, finding a role for newly minted asset classes and securities, and so on. In such an environment, the "cream rises to the top"; the talents, experiences, and ambitions of successful market participants create knowledge and lessons that benefit all participants. This proceedings is the product of an AIMR seminar designed to impart a sampling of that knowledge and those lessons, to explore new tools and new applications of familiar tools—all aimed at answering one of the boldest of investment questions: Is a particular stock fairly valued?

Specifically, this proceedings addresses three key topics with respect to the current state of equity valuation.
- *Information base*: How useful are the research and information disseminated by Wall Street firms? Can equity investors go beyond traditional information sources to support their decision-making processes?
- *Earnings and cash flows*: How can investors assess the quality of earnings and the quality of management? Can traditional accounting-based equity valuation methods be used in creative ways? How does a focus on cash flows avoid problems associated with a focus on earnings?

- *New valuation approaches*: What insights can equity investors gain by using economic value added analysis? What are the advantages and disadvantages of using present value methodologies to value stocks? How can the sales-driven franchise-value framework help investors look at a company in new ways?

Taken together, these topics create the platform from which the authors challenge investors to think about the philosophy and context that does, or should, drive equity valuation. Considered separately, each topic provides a forum in which the authors bring their considerable insights to bear on specific, and often troubling, elements of the valuation process, such as quality of information, nature of key inputs, and choice of approach.

Information Base

Information, whether research findings, accounting data, or company rumors, is the grist for the equity valuation mill, and thoughtful valuation must always question the quality and sufficiency of that information.

Wall Street brokerage firms spend huge amounts of time and money disseminating investment research and recommendations. Timothy Timura examines recent empirical conclusions with respect to the usefulness and market impact of that information. Although the evidence is not overwhelming and certainly not unanimous, Timura concludes that investors can use analysts' advice to earn abnormal returns as well as to discern and use market expectations. He also offers valuable advice about dealing with the conflicts of interest that are inherent in the Wall Street research process.

All investment research activities are built on information, but Kemp Dolliver argues that what distinguishes exceptional research from average research is the use of creative intelligence-gathering techniques. Such techniques have several important uses in the equity valuation process but may well take the equity analyst far afield from the usual information base. Thus, creative intelligence gathering requires that new people and groups be contacted and new sources be plumbed for useful information. Dolliver provides helpful tips for using contact time efficiently and structuring questions effectively and gives several examples of the benefits of creative intelligence gathering.

Earnings and Cash Flows

Corporate earnings and dividends have long served as the basis for traditional equity valuation, but even these tried-and-true techniques can be applied in new and interesting ways. And beyond earnings, cash flow may be an even better measure for relating company performance to stock price.

Fred Speece advocates a "whole brain" approach to equity analysis—one that incorporates both financial (left-brain) and cultural and emotional (right-brain) aspects of the valuation task. Left-brain analysis targets the quality of the company's earnings, defined by Speece to include earnings surprise and consensus and various accounting items and trends. Right-brain analysis emphasizes the quality of management and focuses in particular on the unique culture of the company and the emotional factors that drive both the company's prospects and the valuation of those prospects.

Stock valuation is about judgment between the extremes of cheap and expensive, says Thomas Martin, and traditional equity valuation methods—such as the price-to-book, price-to-sales, and price-to-earnings ratios and the dividend discount model—are ways of exercising that judgment. Martin illustrates two particularly useful applications of these methods: screening and fundamental analysis. In the process, he focuses on the critical interaction of growth and discount rates and advocates the use of two measures (price-implied growth and growth duration) that are not part of many traditional equity valuation approaches.

James Ohlson contends that focusing on cash flow, although not the "cure all" for valuation problems, sharpens many aspects of equity valuation. He sets forth a basic framework for analyzing free cash flow and provides a frank assessment of the benefits and limitations of such a framework. Frustration engendered by those limitations might lead investors back to an earnings-based approach, but Ohlson is convinced that a focus on earnings is even more questionable than a focus on cash flows. He concludes by illustrating free cash flow analysis in a stock valuation context.

New Valuation Approaches

Although often decried as "ivory tower" constructs, theoretical models brought to bear on real practitioner needs can result in powerful new solutions to a prob-

lem. Such is the case with nontraditional equity valuation approaches that define value in new ways and that draw on concepts such as economic value added and present value.

Alfred Jackson believes that investors can use the concept of economic value added (EVA) to enhance equity analysis in a number of ways. Do incremental returns on invested capital exceed the company's cost of capital? Do high-return business units subsidize low-return units? Which geographical operations or business segments create value for a company? EVA analysis can answer all these questions and more. Most importantly, Jackson concludes, EVA is particularly well suited for identifing which stocks are likely to outperform the market.

Globalization is bringing unparalleled complexity and challenges to the investment environment, observes Patrick O'Donnell, and present value methodologies for equity valuation (two high-profile examples being EVA and discounted cash flow) are particularly appealing in such an environment. He provides a comprehensive survey of the state of the art in applying these methodologies—their appeal, advantages and disadvantages, potential benefits, and implementation problems. The widespread adoption of present-value-based valuation tools is likely but not assured, O'Donnell concludes. What is certain is that such tools can improve valuation judgments.

Martin Leibowitz concludes this proceedings by taking a fresh look at the components that determine the value of a company. He shows that total, or intrinsic, value is the sum of tangible value (derived from current business) and franchise value (derived from future business). But this analysis shares with the more traditional approaches an emphasis on earnings. Therefore, Leibowitz recasts the framework to focus on sales rather than earnings; the key component in this sales-driven franchise-value model is the franchise margin, which, as Leibowitz illustrates, can serve as the basis for a valuation model and for restating traditional valuation ratios.

Conclusion

What final message should readers take from this proceedings? What lessons do these gifted authors impart? Yes, equity valuation is probably more difficult now than at any time in its long evolution. However gaining an edge is not only possible but likely if the right information is used, if traditional models are applied in clever ways, and if the best of new approaches is adopted to augment proven valuation methods.

Is Wall Street Research Useful?

Timothy J. Timura, CFA
Portfolio Manager
Pilgrim Baxter Value Investors, Inc.

Does Wall Street research help investors earn abnormal returns? Empirical evidence suggests ways in which investors can use such research and the resulting investment recommendations to discern market expectations and avoid distortions created by potential conflicts of interest.

Wall Street brokerage firms spend an extraordinary amount of time and resources collecting, analyzing, and publishing research and recommendations. Not surprisingly, since Cowles published "Can Stock Market Forecasters Forecast?" in 1933, debate has continued about whether those recommendations do in fact produce abnormal returns. Although the totality of the evidence is mixed, concluding that Wall Street research is not useful in some form would be naive or irrational. To give justice to the issues surrounding the debate, this presentation discusses recent empirical conclusions on the usefulness and market impact of Wall Street research, outlines how investors can discern and effectively and efficiently use Wall Street expectations, and addresses potential analyst conflicts of interest.

Empirical Conclusions

Some of the recent academic literature reports empirical conclusions that provide insight into the potential use of Wall Street research. Womack (1996) studied market reaction and security return behavior associated with analyst recommendations and reached the following conclusions:

- Recommendations by the top 14 largest brokerage firms are predominantly issued on well-followed, large-capitalization stocks.
- The ratio of new buy to new sell recommendations is approximately seven to one.
- The six-month mean return prior to a new recommendation, either a buy or sell, is *not* significantly different from zero, but for stocks that are being withdrawn from recommendation lists, the prior six-month return *is* significantly different from zero and in the direction previously forecast by analysts. That is, the stock price is

essentially unchanged prior to a new recommendation, but if the recommendation is changed, the stock generally outperforms the market if the change is buy to sell and generally underperforms the market if the change is sell to buy.

- The three-day recommendation period returns are significant and in the direction forecast by analysts.
- Postrecommendation excess returns are not mean reverting but are significant and in the direction forecast by analysts. For added-to-buy recommendation changes, the excess return occurs predominantly in the first postrecommendation month; for added-to-sell changes, the excess return accrues over roughly six months.
- The market reaction to added-to-buy and added-to-sell recommendations is asymmetric. Market responses to new sell recommendations are of greater magnitude than responses to new buy recommendations, both in the three-day event period and in the six-month postrecommendation drift period.
- The market reaction associated with small-cap firms is significantly larger than that associated with large-cap firms, both in the recommendation period and in the postrecommendation event days.

Stickel's (1992) findings complement a number of Womack's conclusions. Stickel compared *Institutional Investor* All-America Research Team members with other analysts on the basis of three factors: forecast accuracy, frequency of forecast issuance, and impact of forecast revisions on security prices. Stickel concluded that members of the All-America Research Team supply more-accurate earnings forecasts, and with greater frequency, than other analysts. Patterns of stock returns immediately following large upward forecast revisions suggest that these recommendations from the All-America Research Team affect stock prices more than do other analysts' upward recommendations; however, Stickel found no difference between large downward revisions from the All-America Research Team and those from other analysts. Furthermore, he found that the impact of revisions on prices is generally positively related to the change in forecast and is generally greater for small firms than large firms. Stickel's collective evidence suggests a positive relationship between "reputation," as measured by *Institutional Investor*, and performance.

Taken together, the Womack and Stickel conclusions provide strong evidence that stock prices are influenced by analysts' recommendation changes, not only at the immediate time of the announcement but also in subsequent months. The most puzzling finding of the Womack study is that, even though the near-term reactions are large, they appear to be incomplete, showing nontrivial postrecommendation drift.

Regarding postrecommendation drift, Abarbanell and Bernard (1992) examined whether security analysts underreact or overreact to prior earnings information. They presented evidence that analysts' forecasts underreact to recent earnings information *and* that the underreactions in forecasts are at most only half as large as necessary to substantiate the postrecommendation or the postevent drift. Therefore, Abarbanell and Bernard suggested that an explanation of this anomaly may rest in an understanding of why even professional analysts in apparently competitive markets tend to make systematic errors in earnings forecasting. Such evidence could reflect psychological forces that cause people who are making predictions to place too little weight on recent changes in a series—what the behavioral finance theorists call "anchoring"—or could even be induced by the incentive structure faced by professional analysts. Before analysts are too unfairly judged, however, evidence suggests that stock prices (i.e., the investment community) appear to react to the earnings news with even more delay than do the analysts' estimates.

In addition to analyst underreaction, Abarbanell and Bernard raised the issue of analyst overreaction. Assuming that the behaviorists are correct and that overreactions do occur in the market, the question is: What is driving the overreactions? Some academics have suggested that stock market participants may be overreacting to current earnings changes by not recognizing that extreme revisions tend to be partially reversed in the future. Abarbanell and Bernard's message is that analysts' "generalized overreaction," as popularized by De Bondt and Thaler (1990), is not

easily viewed as an overreaction to earnings and not clearly connected to overreactions in stock prices. This finding suggests that the long-term reversals in stock prices discussed by De Bondt and Thaler can be understood by looking at a factor (some unspecified information or psychological source) other than simply "extreme" earnings-induced analyst behavior.

LaPorta (1996), for instance, argued that analyst expectations about *future growth* in earnings are too extreme. Specifically, LaPorta sorted stocks by expected growth rates in earnings—defined as five-year forecasts—and found that low-growth-expectation stocks beat high-growth-expectation stocks by 20 percentage points over a five-year period. Following are his conclusions:

- In the year following initiation of the long-term growth forecast, analysts revise, sometimes sharply, their expectations about the level of earnings and the rate of growth in earnings in the direction predicted by an errors-in-expectations hypothesis.
- For high-growth-expectation stocks, large errors in analysts' forecasts of the level of earnings show up as early as the next fiscal year.
- Generally, event study evidence suggests that the market is overly pessimistic about the earnings of the low-growth-expectation portfolios and excessively optimistic about the earnings of the high-growth-expectation portfolios.

In essence, LaPorta's extrapolation hypothesis holds that, although it takes time for analysts to become aware of new trends, once they do, many analysts latch onto these perceived trends for far too long.

In summary, the empirical evidence suggests that analysts are somewhat slow to react to new earnings information, but when they do react, they tend to overly extrapolate long-term growth rates. The fact remains, however, that investors can earn abnormal returns by trading in the direction of changes in analysts' advice.

Discerning Expectations

If studies are correct in their conclusions that Wall Street information is useful, then investors should be able to use that information in several ways to discern market expectations.

■ *Industry analysis and perspective.* Given their specific (i.e., narrow) coverage responsibilities, Wall Street analysts have a virtually unparalleled perspective on industry dynamics; they have uniquely comprehensive access to trade associations, government statistics, company managements, competitors, and investment bankers. In short, Wall Street research can help build a bottom-up and a top-down industry backdrop for stock selection.

■ *Balance sheet, income statement, and cash flow statement generation.* Using a wealth of sources, Wall Street analysts spend a great deal of time building company financial forecasts. In the name of efficiency, investors should not reinvent the wheel; rather, they can simply leverage already prepared financial statements by adjusting those financials to reflect their own research inputs, insights, and perspectives. With the new online access arrangements, this method can be a real time-saver for the analytical process.

■ *Historical analysis.* Because of familiarity with their respective universes, Wall Street analysts can offer investors the opportunity to profit from a historical perspective. Wall Street analysts are uniquely positioned to help assess the integrity of a company's management, to analyze management's pronouncements and guidance, and to provide a balanced story in response to a revisionist management's effort at "spin control."

■ *Sounding board.* Wall Street analysts have proved to be a rational sounding board for thoughts, questions, and "what-if" scenarios. Their perspectives, especially those resulting from their extensive contacts, can be assessed for a reality check against investors' own thoughts.

Using Expectational Information

Analysis, perspective, reality check—all are important uses of Wall Street information, but the real question is: How do investors tie all of this information together in an effort to effectively and efficiently use Wall Street inputs to generate an excess return in the market?

The key drivers of stock prices are all expectational. Accordingly, investors can attempt to tie the Wall Street research and interactions together to develop a proxy for market expectations concerning
- growth dynamics (sales growth, earnings growth rate, cash flow dynamics),
- financial objectives (return on equity, return on equity targets, economic value added dynamics, free cash flow, gross margins),
- corporate actions (product development, acquisitions, divestitures, dividends),
- economic variables (interest rates, inflation, Federal Reserve policy, risk premiums), and
- market participants (other buy-side firms, hedge funds).

Then, in combination with a given valuation methodology, knowledge of the significant empirical research outlined earlier, and an understanding of the psychology of market participants, investors can isolate, frame, and assess the reality and the pricing of the pertinent expectations that drive returns.

A classic example of the potentially profitable use of this assessment of expectations occurred with bank stocks in early 1991. Because of the difficult and uncertain near-term economic and credit environment, most Wall Street analysts and investors were extrapolating the then-current weak fundamentals into the foreseeable future and were very cautious in their 1991 and 1992 earnings projections, five-year earnings growth rate forecasts, and return on equity (ROE) forecasts. In short, expectations surrounding bank stocks were grim. Valuation analysis that focused on P/E and price-to-book multiples *confirmed* that bank stocks were discounting abnormally low earnings growth rates and ROE levels.

A review of history, however, would have suggested that bank earnings, growth rates, and ROEs rebound solidly in an economic recovery, especially one that benefits from an openly accommodative Federal Reserve policy stance. Additionally, industry conferences and management discussions were focusing on the corrective steps being taken to enhance future prospects, and thus, they were not as pessimistic about the group's fundamentals as the analysts were.

Bank stocks in 1991 were a classic case of expectations being too pessimistic, a case that allowed the opportunistic investor to make selective purchases that have proven to be among the best in the 1990s.

Conflicts of Interest

Any party to a business transaction must always evaluate how or why the other party in that transaction is compensated. Although obviously firm specific, Wall Street analysts' compensation packages generally depend on the following factors:
- evaluation by the brokerage sales force,
- standing in the *Institutional Investor* poll,
- job market conditions and potential job offers from competitors,
- investment banking business generated, because investment banking fees may be as much as 30–40 percent of a research division's budget,
- trading volume in recommended stocks, and
- success of buy and sell recommendations.

In short, because of multiple compensation sources, the Wall Street analyst serves many masters and constituencies. So, what may appear to be a conflict of interest to one constituency is not to another.

Investors would do well to remember the "consenting adults theory"—that is, one enters into a business situation willingly and with eyes wide open. An investor would have to be naive or irrational to believe that the analyst, the management, the trader, the portfolio manager, or the investment banker on the other side of the table is *not* operating first and foremost with his or her own interests in mind. Consequently, an investor who distrusts someone on the other side of the table should not engage in any activity with that party; no one is being coerced.

On the specific issue of conflicts related to investment banking relationships, the buy side's skepticism regarding the sell side's investment banking relationships is fairly well based. As in almost any business transaction, the various parties will have conflicts of interest. Understanding this fact allows both parties to proceed intelligently and openly with transactions that can benefit their respective constituents.

Conclusion

Fortunately, to be successful in the investment business, participants need to make their own decisions and then take responsibility for the outcome. The business of investments should involve playing a calculated set of odds and using all available resources to add abnormal returns. Investors should be solidifying an unassailable investment philosophy and process that is theoretically based, empirically testable, and intuitively appealing. It should also appropriately leverage unique strengths and resources; the resource base unarguably should include Wall Street research.

References

Abarbanell, Jeffery S., and Victor L. Bernard. 1992. "Tests of Analysts' Overreaction/Underreaction to Earnings Information as an Explanation for Anomalous Stock Price Behavior." *Journal of Finance* (July):1181–1206.

Cowles, Alfred. 1933. "Can Stock Market Forecasters Forecast?" *Econometrica* (July):309–24.

De Bondt, Werner F.M., and Richard Thaler. 1990. "Do Security Analysts Overreact?" *American Economic Review* (May):52–57.

LaPorta, Rafael. 1996. "Expectations and the Cross-Section of Stock Returns." *Journal of Finance* (December):1715–41.

Stickel, Scott E. 1992. "Reputation and Performance among Security Analysts." *Journal of Finance* (December):1811–36.

Womack, Kent L. 1996. "Do Brokerage Analysts' Recommendations Have Investment Value?" *Journal of Finance* (March):137–65.

Question and Answer Session

Timothy J. Timura, CFA

Question: Do analysts rely heavily on companies' forecasts of earnings and profitability?

Timura: My participation in many conference calls and my study of analysts' research suggests that analysts depend somewhat on management's guidance. The better analysts take that company information, meld it with all their other sources (including other conference calls, other management's input, and other competitors' information), and generate estimates or forecasts that are different, either better or worse, from the company's own general guidance. These "amalgamated" estimates are some of the most valuable research pieces that come across my desk.

Question: Should there be changes in the rules of disclosure for Street analysts when their firm is the banker?

Timura: The rules are clear: Every report on a company for which the issuing firm has acted as a banker or advisor must contain a disclosure note revealing that role. In that context, we simply enter into any discussion or dialog with a high degree of skepticism and cynicism.

Question: Do analysts' changes in earnings estimates prior to reported earnings have an impact on stock price?

Timura: Yes. Using earnings revision, surprise, and momentum has become widespread. Interevent or interperiod changes in analysts' estimates are, therefore, very important to a large number of professional investors.

Question: Why does Wall Street not issue more sell recommendations? What, if anything, will change that?

Timura: First, to the latter question. In the past 15 years, the market has gone in only one direction. In a standard bear market, one will probably observe more sell recommendations. As to why there are fewer sell recommendations, there are several reasons. First, investment banking relationships (present and future) could be jeopardized; second, top management and investor relation contacts may limit or cut off information; and third, reputational injury from an incorrect sell recommendation is high because of the high visibility.

Question: Please address the importance of whisper forecasts on the Street.

Timura: Whisper numbers have become a lot more pronounced in the 1990s than they ever were in the 1980s, partly because of better information dissemination. In a world where a number of participants are looking at the concept of earnings revision, earnings surprise, and earnings momentum, whisper forecasts become an important component and allow us to lean in the direction of the positive revisions and positive surprises. I would caution, however, that investors have to evaluate many of those whispers in the context of the expectations already embedded in the stock price. In a number of instances, I have heard whisper numbers and seen a stock rise, and then, after the earnings number has come out in excess of that "whisper" number, the stock price has gone down.

Creative Intelligence Gathering

B. Kemp Dolliver, CFA
Vice President
Cowen & Company

What distinguishes exceptional from average investment research is the use of creative intelligence-gathering techniques. But productive use of such techniques requires a special skill set—knowing the people and groups to contact and where to look for information, using contact time efficiently, and posing the right questions in the right way.

Information, and thus information gathering, is the glue that holds together any research effort, including investment management research. In this high-tech era, everyone has access to a plethora of data sources, but what distinguishes exceptional from average research is the use of creative intelligence-gathering techniques.

This presentation defines and sets the context for creative intelligence gathering and then identifies potential sources for intelligence gathering—the people and groups to contact and the places to look for information. The later sections of the presentation contain tips for using a contact's time and for posing questions, as well as some examples of the benefits of conducting creative intelligence gathering.

Definition

The standard procedure for researching a potential investment involves three steps. First, look at the financial statements and understand the numbers. Second, talk to the company itself; get management's perspective on the industry and current business trends. Third, understand the business: Talk to the people working on Wall Street to get a broad perspective on what is going on within the industry. By following those steps, analysts come to understand the consensus view on a stock, what the expectations are, and perhaps who holds the stock and how it trades.

Creative intelligence gathering is everything that is not included in those three steps. It involves all the other sources of information that exist but generally are not readily available. The information is not on the front page of the *Wall Street Journal*, and it is not for sale from Wall Street. In other words, this information is gathered outside the usual channels. It is sometimes proprietary, it may be material, and it can be immensely valuable.

Uses

Creative intelligence gathering addresses the typical informational needs of analysts and investors—needs that take one of three forms.

■ *Decision making.* When trying to make an immediate buy or sell recommendation, for example, creative intelligence gathering can help fill in the decision mosaic more clearly and with more depth. It can provide additional understanding of the company or the security. By evaluating a company's performance relative to its industry or peer group, analysts can develop better assessments of the sustainability of the company's results.

■ *Enhanced understanding.* Even when an immediate need does not exist for the information, it will enhance understanding of the company or security in the long term. Suppose as analysts we are very interested in a company, but the stock looks expensive and we have some concerns about the stock that we think may surface in the future. Thus, we do not want to purchase the stock now. Creative intelligence gathering can help us learn what is going on; hopefully, we will know a little more than everybody else in the market does. If a controversy does arise with the stock, then we can take advantage of that additional information, and of other people's mistakes, at the proper time.

■ *Idea generation.* Creative intelligence gathering can be very helpful when looking for new ideas. Today's business world is an interrelated one in which companies deal with each other as competitors, suppliers, and customers. Trends in one company are probably being reflected elsewhere, and creative intelligence gathering can help find the not-so-obvious plays, the stocks that are not in the middle of every analyst's radar screen. For example, a large company that is raising prices in one of its smaller business lines may create an investment opportunity in a smaller competitor with much more exposure to that market.

Sources: Whom to Contact

One of the most difficult, but necessary, tasks in creative intelligence gathering is determining whom to contact for particular kinds of information. Fortunately, the potential sources are many and varied.

■ *Competitors.* When researching a company, we should talk to some of its competitors to get a broad perspective on the industry: what the issues are, how the competitive dynamics line up, who the high end/low end market players are. This perspective provides a framework for comparison when one company may be saying something about the industry but another company is saying something else. As analysts, we need to have that industrywide perspective to determine who has the accurate story.

■ *Industry contacts.* Contacts at privately held companies, who do not have stocks to promote, can be very helpful, especially if such companies are large and have a good reputation. Developing that type of relationship and dialog is extremely helpful. Contacts at privately held companies can be objective about what is going on in the industry and may have more time to talk than others because they do not have Wall Street calling them constantly. Private companies can be found through trade group directories and even the yellow pages, depending on the industry.

■ *Trade groups.* Another source of valuable information is trade groups, which provide services to their membership that can be extremely useful for analysts. For instance, many provide statistics that show how an industry has behaved over the years and what kind of growth rate the industry has had. Those data help supply a broad perspective on the industry. Trade groups also have membership directories that indicate who the players are beyond the ones that have high visibility. In addition, trade groups sponsor conferences and trade shows, which can be worth attending. Trade groups may also have their own publications about the industry or about pertinent legislative and regulatory activities.

A company can tell us if it belongs to a trade group, and some companies cite data from trade groups in the industry discussion piece of their 10-Ks. Telephone directories are another potential source for locating information about trade groups, as are directories of trade groups themselves.

■ *Consultants.* Consultants can be helpful, especially small consulting firms that specialize by industry. In many cases, these firms are run by people who have left an industry, some of whom established good reputations in that industry. In addition, accountants, doctors, lawyers, or any other professionals who have specialized knowledge in a field can help fill in any gaps in our understanding. Some consulting firms publish newsletters and studies. These publications and studies are often expensive, but sometimes they are quite reasonably priced. Essentially, consultants are selling their time and resources. We may be able to afford what they have to sell, and we may not. At least we should make the effort to find out what is available.

■ *Lobbyists.* Many industries are subject to extensive regulatory and legislative activity. Having contacts in the lobbyist community can help to monitor legislation and to understand how companies are actually behaving in crafting legislation. Because all companies in an industry may not have the same interests legislatively, they may compete with each other in crafting legislation. Knowing that fact helps us understand how those companies view the business. So, in an industry that is highly influenced by government action, seeing how companies behave relative to each other can be enlightening.

■ *Regulators.* Simply put, the regulators make the rules. In the utility business, for example, they tell companies how much they can earn. In the drug business, regulators tell companies when they can bring a drug to market. Regulators probably will not sit and talk to us directly. But by getting to know the process, we can understand how regulators should and do make decisions, assuming that everything is rational and that we have a good picture of the process. That understanding can be extremely helpful in making appropriate forecasts of regulatory decisions and actions.

In addition, regulators are data mills, because they have to understand the financial dynamics of the industries they regulate. They collect and process volumes of data from companies and industries. In general, all the data are available to the public. This information is worth digging out to get a perspective on how regulators view what the companies are doing, which may be something they do not talk about. I once spent part of an afternoon researching a telephone rate case in Connecticut, one aspect of which was particularly enlightening. I looked at the dockets of who attended the rate hearing meetings. Typically, the regulators greatly outnumbered the company representatives, which indicated the regulatory mindset: The regulators had a lot of people dedicated to a process to which the companies could dedicate only a few people. From this exercise, I developed an appreciation for the sluggishness of the regulatory process.

■ *Reporters.* Good reporters are helpful contacts. They can tell us where to find information they use in their stories, such as a regulatory filing or a certain document. Sometimes reporters can give us tips on where to find information because they are trying to find the same documents themselves. Reporters will not necessarily tell us who they are quoting, but they can tell us where to find some independent data.

The press often has access to people that Wall Street has no access to, either because the reporter has a relationship with a particular contact or because the company is in a situation where management access is controlled. In those situations, particularly in the case of controlled management access, talking to a reporter off the record about how a person sounds can be helpful. I once heard a reporter say, "I have been talking to Mr. X for the past couple of months, and he sounds more exhausted every time we talk." In this case, Mr. X was not showing up in the public eye much and his company was in a crisis, so this input from the reporter was helpful for understanding how things were going internally at the company.

■ *Investor contacts.* Investor relations people are one of the standard sources of information, but the better we can get to know them and their backgrounds, the better the dialog we can have—a dialog that extends beyond "how is the business" and "what does the quarter look like?" The investor relations people in different companies talk to each other; they have a trade group that brings them together across industries. Because of these interindustry contacts, a lot of these people are knowledgeable in areas beyond the narrow focus of their company or industry.

Depending on the company, investor relations people may come from a line of business within the company, instead of from a strict financial background, and may have a hands-on understanding of what is going on in the company. For example, I have a contact at a health care company in Philadelphia. The company has multiple product lines, and my contact came up through one of the divisions. One of the mistakes I have made over the years has been to ignore some of what he has said about one of the company's competitors; he has warned me, correctly, about some of the competitor's problems, and I should have listened.

Distinguishing between investor relations people who are telling us what they know and those who are telling us what they are told to tell us is often difficult. To a large extent, we can alleviate this problem by doing our own homework. The investor contact who sounds like the Wall Street analyst is not adding much value to the discussion. We need to get some other information against which we can do a litmus test. We need to do some comparative work and talk to several companies and an industry contact. Out of a broad range of contacts, some will simply give the company line, but some will be helpful, telling us what they are really thinking.

Sources: Where to Look

Not all creative intelligence gathering is done person-to-person; useful information is also available by conducting old-fashioned research through numerous sources, many of which are inexpensive and easily accessible.

■ *Libraries.* Public libraries maintain subscriptions to a wide range of periodicals, most of which are industry focused. For example, the Boston Public Library has about 500–600 magazines and journals covering a broad range of topics. A few of those publications may be worth subscribing to or at least worth monitoring. Not everybody has access to a large public library, but colleges and business schools also have good libraries and access is often free. Conducting research in this manner is a matter of going in, perusing the journals, and looking at articles to understand what is going on in a particular company or industry. As analysts, we want to know whether the information in the journals is different from what Wall Street is indicating and/or different from what the companies are saying. Library research can be a significant investment in time, but it is worth the time, especially when it is impossible to subscribe to journals at the office.

■ *Publications.* Pay attention to the people quoted in publications. In articles in the *Wall Street Journal* or *Barron's*, we often see familiar people quoted—company officers, Wall Street analysts, regulatory officials, and so on. Occasionally, we learn about people who are not in the usual "cast of characters." We may find out about some well-regarded industry consultants or some people in the business who are not at management levels but are in the "trenches" of the business. We should try to call these people. If they will talk to a reporter, they probably will be willing to talk to us, especially if we are calling to get more information on what they were quoted about in the press. For a lot of people, being quoted is a flattering experience; an even more flattering experience is to have someone notice the quote. So, most people in this situation would be happy to talk to us.

Industry-specific publications are helpful because they are focused and information often appears in the trade press earlier than it appears in the general media (sometimes, the information may not appear in the general media at all). At times, we can catch turning points in industry fundamentals by watching the trade press closely because it is so focused. Industry-specific publications also provide a broad perspective on the players because they talk to companies that are under Wall Street's watchful eye and other constituencies that may not have a public market voice.

The trade press and other media at times contain references to various studies done either by the government, which are free, or consulting groups, which can range from free to expensive. When we see something of interest in the press, we should follow it up with a phone call. We may be able to get a report that is out of date for less than the original price, or we may be able to get it for free because we are not part of the consultant's normal customer base.

Finally, we should look not only at the articles in trade publications; we should also look at the advertisements. We may find some phone numbers for people or companies we want to call. We should also look for ads for the companies we follow to see their products and how they are positioning their products: Are the ads consistent with the story they tell us about how this product should be perceived, and received, in the marketplace? For example, I saw an advertisement promoting uses of avocado in a restaurant trade magazine. The ad claimed that by putting avocado on a sandwich, the restaurant could call it a Mexican sandwich and charge an extra dollar. The ad further claimed that the gross margin on such a use was about 90 percent; this information is a useful tidbit for a restaurant analyst.

■ *Internet.* Searching the Internet can take up large chunks of time, but it is useful. A wide array of companies, trade groups, consulting firms, and government agencies have World Wide Web sites. These sites vary widely in usefulness: Some will have interesting information; some will not. For instance, some consulting firms post examples of their recent work on the Internet. Normally, consultants charge hundreds or thousands of dollars for this work, but they might post a recent report to attract potential customers. The point is to learn who the industry players are, see if they have a Web site, and see what is there.

The U.S. Congress and most agencies of the federal government have Web sites that make a wealth of information and data available. For example, the Web site *Thomas*, which can be found at http://thomas.loc.gov, has almost all of the legislative activity occurring on Capitol Hill at any given point in time. But other Web sites also cover legislative activity. (If exact Web site addresses are not readily available, the site address is often the agency's acronym followed by ".gov".) For instance,

when I was researching the Balanced Budget Act for information about Medicare reimbursement to hospitals, I looked at *Thomas* and found a description filled with legalese. The American Hospital Association had a summary on its Web site of the Balanced Budget Act and its impact on hospitals that was very readable. We need to understand the sources that are available and determine which are the best suited for a particular purpose.

■ *Merger proxies.* Selling a business is a significant event in a company's history, and presumably, management has approached it with a thorough analysis of the company's prospects, the business's value, and where the industry is headed. Therefore, merger proxies are useful documents for conducting creative intelligence gathering on a company. These documents are thick and do not need to be read from cover to cover; rather, focusing on just a few sections will usually yield needed information.

For instance, merger proxies provide the background of the deal—why the company is selling. Frequently, this section is boilerplate language, but in some instances, interesting opinions from management with regard to where the business is going can be found in this section. For example, in 1994, several deals involved a number of the smaller health maintenance organizations (HMOs). I know of at least two instances in which management cited concerns about the competitive environment as a reason for selling the company. If investors had used that information and reduced their positions, or gotten out of that industry altogether, they would have avoided several years of underperformance by that industry. So, we need to pay attention to why managements are making these decisions to sell, because they should be approaching such decisions with some degree of seriousness. We may get some insight into what is going on that we would not get elsewhere.

A merger proxy also shows how managements behave. It contains a description of the sale process—who contacted whom, how the deal progressed. It does not have all the details, but if we have enough perspective on the industry, we may be able to read between the lines and see who else may have surfaced as a potential buyer, or we may be able to uncover why certain decisions were made. To the extent that management is staying in the business, merger proxies can help us understand how they view the process.

In addition, we need to keep in mind that management does not always act in shareholders' interests. Sometimes management's interests may end up ahead of shareholders'. If these managers come back to the public market with other companies, we will know something about their track records.

Finally, merger proxies contain information on

the fair market values of comparable companies, usually found in the section titled "Opinion of Financial Advisor." We can take the information, copy it, and file it away. When advisors do a fairness opinion, they typically look at how stocks are traded in the public market based on discounted cash flow. The really interesting data that have some lasting value are the data on previous transactions in the industry: multiples of cash flow, multiples of revenues, and multiples of book value. We can use those data in our evaluation work to determine what kind of upside a stock has. If a company is subject to a tender offer, we can do an instant fairness opinion on our own and get some idea of how this offer compares with previous offers, which is exactly what the managements are trying to do. Even if a deal does not involve a stock we own, if it occurs in an industry that we follow, we should try to get the proxy statement and put it in the file, because the valuation data are relatively timeless.

■ *Government.* David Easton said, "Politics is the authoritative allocation of value," which means government gives and government takes away—perhaps a license or a drug approval. The government's decisions are very important in a number of industries, and understanding and staying current with what the government is thinking and doing are crucial.

The local offices of particular representatives or senators can be good sources of information. Also, most agencies publish catalogs of all the information they generate. Subscriptions are generally free or very inexpensive. For an industry that is subject to a lot of government action, those resources are very useful.

Using a Contact's Time

Following is a quick primer on how to get the maximum benefit in a brief period of time when, as analysts, we are calling somebody we do not know and trying to explain what we are looking for.

■ *Define what is needed.* We should figure out the questions that need to be asked and what kind of information is needed in as concise a manner as possible. By being organized, we can get through the process quickly. Our contact person does not have to speak to us, so we want to use time wisely.

■ *Be straightforward.* We want to start off with a good impression, because we may want to talk to this person again. As a general rule, we should identify ourselves as an investment person up front; we are better off being honest about what we are looking for and who we are. We may quickly explain what we do, but preferably without a lot of detail. When talking to someone who is not financially oriented, we might spend 10 minutes explaining our job and our firm instead of getting the information we need. Also,

we should explain how we found the person. Was that person quoted in the press? Is the person a friend of somebody we know? Leading off with that information can help get the discussion going, but we must quickly and finally get to the point of what we want to know: the information we are seeking and how that person can help us.

■ *Remember sources' potential biases.* We need to keep in mind the biases a contact might have. If the person works at a company that has a particular view of the world, we need to take that fact into account if the information we get does not mesh with what we heard from others or if it is information we did not expect to hear. If we expect the person to have a certain set of biases and he or she tells us something different, that information is probably better than if the person had told us everything we expected to hear, because we are probably getting an honest viewpoint on a topic. If we do not know the contact well enough to know of any biases, we should keep the questions factual in nature.

■ *Ask for another source.* If the person is helpful—he or she spent a lot of time with us and told us what we wanted to know—we should find out if that person knows of anyone else who can help us. We should always be mindful of building the network wider and wider so as to have more people we can turn to when we need to get some information.

■ *Thank profusely.* Genuine thanks go a long way in our business, particularly if we can offer our contact something of interest, such as a brokerage report on a company or even a simple stock chart, because we will probably be remembered for years. We may not talk to all our sources frequently, and if we can provide our contacts with something useful, we will stand out in their minds. When we call again, they will think, "This is the person who did X for me; I remember that person, and he or she is worth talking to."

■ *Do not wait for a crisis to gather information.* If we are trying to gather information in the midst of a crisis, it is probably too late, because reality has likely caught up with perception and it can be very hard to get the information we want quickly. The creative intelligence-gathering process involves making an investment in time and building relationships. We should try to make contacts and forge relationships as part of our normal investment process. On a day when the market is slow, we should try to do some contact building, because it can be very helpful later.

Asking the Right Questions

Deciding what questions to ask is only half the battle. The other half is how to ask the questions—the format and tone necessary to get the information needed.

■ *Null hypothesis.* One technique is to posit a null hypothesis about conditions in an industry or an action somebody has taken and say, "If I am right on all these assumptions, I would have expected this result." Then I can ask the contact person, "Tell me where I am wrong." We want to find out how this person approaches the idea or decision in question. Whether or not the right decision was made is less important than how the decision was made. Some companies are very insightful in their planning processes; that fact may come out only if we ask how they go about making decisions. In this manner, we can also pick up a bit of insight with regard to how the company views the world, which can help forecast how the company will act in the future. Essentially, what we are trying to do is to learn how management thinks. What is the planning process? What is the capital-budgeting process? Does management tend to be loose in its planning? Is management quantitatively oriented? By understanding these nuances, we can learn to forecast what management is doing or, more importantly, what it should be doing strategically.

■ *Similar company.* If we own or are looking at a stock that has encountered problems and we want to understand what should evolve—what are the dynamics—a useful approach is to find another company in the industry that has encountered the same problems in the past and get its perspective on the process. We do not have to ask this second company what it thinks will happen at the first company; we simply need to ask, "What did you go through? How did you make the decisions?" We should stay away from "What do you think will happen at Company X?" or "What do you think of these people at Company X?" because a conflict of interest might be involved. Someone else's weakness may be this company's advantage, and it is best to keep the conversation as objective as possible.

In 1996, Northeast Utilities ran into problems with its nuclear power plants in Connecticut. At the time, the stock looked interesting. I had the opportunity to meet with some people from Baltimore Gas and Electric (BG&E), which had already gone through a long, painful process with its nuclear power facilities and their attendant problems. I asked BG&E what it went through and whether the process would likely be different for Northeast Utilities. BG&E was exactly right in identifying the changes that Northeast Utilities would have to, and did, go through.

■ *Nonhostile environment.* We can ask people the toughest question imaginable if we ask it in a nonhostile manner. I have led off countless questions with "Am I missing something?" or "I do not understand this." By asking a question in this manner, we

put our contact at ease instead of saying "How could you do this?" and putting that person on the defensive. We get better answers when people feel comfortable talking to us, whether on the buy side or sell side. To the extent we need to have relationships with people and have a dialog, it is important to get the information we want without putting someone in the position of wanting to never speak to us again.

Examples

The following examples illustrate how building a network of press and industry contacts allowed me to pursue some creative intelligence gathering, which resulted in some very helpful information.

■ *Press contact.* In August 1995, I was quoted in the local press about the first HMO that had disastrous earnings. A couple of months later, I was contacted by the publisher of a home health newsletter who got my name from that article. He wanted to know about one of the companies that I followed, Columbia HCA Healthcare Corporation, which had just reported earnings. He asked me questions about the home health care business and the statistics that Columbia gave out. Frankly, this was a small piece of the company, and I had not given much thought to it. He proceeded to tell me a little bit about what he was seeing from the industry perspective and even sent me some of his company's publications. Those materials were very interesting, because they discussed the issue of cost shifting by hospitals in the home health agencies, which became one of the core issues for Columbia in 1997. I did not make a "sell" call in 1995 or 1996, but when I saw the 1997 headline "The FBI Has Shown Up in El Paso," we sold quickly. We did not know everything that was going on, but we had a sense that this was probably the start of something bigger and worse, which turned out to be the right insight.

■ *Workshop contact.* That same 1995 article in which I was quoted provided me with a helpful contact who helped me make a valuable investment decision. Because of the article, I was contacted by the local medical society and asked to participate in a two-day workshop that they sponsored to get people to understand what doctors go through with regard to managed care. One of the people I followed around was a surgeon, which paid off for me because I was looking at a company that had a new surgical product coming to market. I called the surgeon and said, "I want to get your perspective on how useful this product will be." His perspective on the product was more conservative than the company's forecast, so I stopped working on the stock, which turned out to be the right decision.

■ *Industry contact.* In early 1994, I met with the chief financial officer of a healthcare real estate investment trust. I asked him an innocent question: "Are you looking at any new facilities outside your core nursing home business?" He said, "Yes, I am looking at something entirely new: children's detention centers. We have come into contact with a company (Children's Comprehensive Services), and we are going to give them a loan to finance some of their facilities. They provide services to state and local governments for troubled youths and adolescents." Children's Comprehensive Services was on the verge of bankruptcy, but he was very excited about it. His company was putting money up and taking a financial risk.

His comments led me to do some work on this stock. At the time, 1994, the stock was trading around $4–$5 a share, as shown in **Figure 1**. This company was not being followed by any analysts, but one of the funds at the company I was working at took a small position. The numbers improved, the turnaround ensued, and then the momentum crowd came in and took the stock up to about $24 a share in May 1996. It has not done as well since then, but over three years,

it has increased in value about fourfold. So, that one simple question back in 1994 led to some valuable information and a good investment decision.

Conclusion

Creative intelligence gathering has some very tangible benefits. First, the better informed we are as investors, the better decisions we should make. The investment management business is a business with conflicting and incomplete information and a lot of pressure to process and use that information quickly. To the extent we understand what is going on, we can take more intelligently measured risks. Second, information can be timeless in its value and usefulness. Keeping track of what we have picked up, people we have talked to, and things they have said might not have immediate value but may have future value in unexpected ways. Finally, by conducting creative intelligence gathering, we can avoid being at the mercy of biases—our own and other people's—and of the vagaries of market speculation.

Figure 1. Children's Comprehensive Services: Monthly Stock Price, January 1994–November 1997

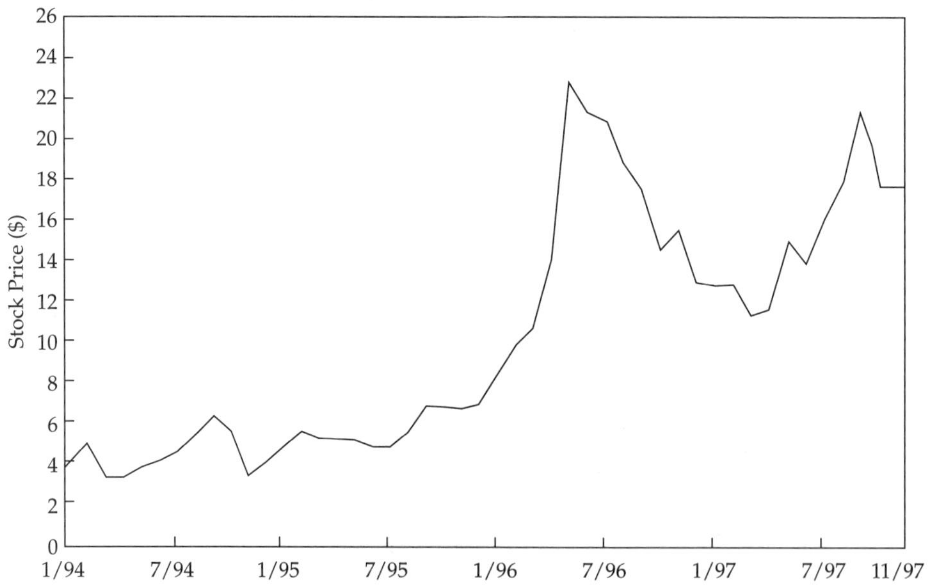

Source: Based on data from ILX Systems.

Question and Answer Session

B. Kemp Dolliver, CFA

Question: How do you get small companies to return your calls?

Dolliver: If I am persistent and a company still does not call me back, obviously, the company is sending me a message. The only way around that situation is to find somebody who can give me entry to that company.

Question: How do you motivate unrelated parties to answer your questions?

Dolliver: I have not encountered too much resistance in that regard once I get somebody on the phone. Some of it may be a function of who you work for. I have had the benefit of working for some large, well-known organizations, which sometimes makes a difference in terms of getting people to talk. But

a lot of overcoming resistance boils down to persistence.

Question: Where do you get timely data about insider trading?

Dolliver: Timely filing is one of the great unenforced rules of insider trading. I see what is in the *Wall Street Journal* and what is available through InvestNet or some of the third-party services that track insider trading closely.

Question: How much time do you allocate to creative information gathering?

Dolliver: It is hard to measure because the work ebbs and flows, but I would say at least 10–15 percent of my time is devoted to creative information gathering. It depends somewhat on what I am

trying to do. If I am neutral or negative on a stock that I think has a lot of problems, I will probably spend less time looking for information about that stock versus a stock I am recommending.

Question: What are the critical variables that drive stocks from the perspective of creative intelligence gathering?

Dolliver: The critical variable is consistency with expectations. If the market has a view of a company and its prospects and we are getting information that is substantially different from that view (either better or worse), that insight will lead to realized outperformance or underperformance at some point.

Assessing the Quality of Earnings and Management

Fred H. Speece, Jr., CFA
Founder
Speece, Lewis & Thorson, Inc.

Creative analysis of the quality of a company's earnings and its management requires both sides of an analyst's brain. The left brain looks at purely financial aspects (e.g., earnings consensus and surprises, accounting conventions and trends), and the right brain focuses on cultural features and emotional factors that are embedded in a company's prospects.

As analysts, we are always trying to find a better way to analyze companies and make investment judgments. During the past 10–15 years, the United States has had a great investment environment. Inflation and interest rates have been declining, and earnings and valuation multiples have been rising dramatically; thus, most analysts' judgments appear to have been successful. But now, earnings growth and the valuation-multiple expansion may well have run their course, and we will need to work smarter to identify those investments that will continue to excel without the benefit of a rising tide of earnings and multiples.

One approach to working smarter is the use of whole brain analysis. Whole brain analysis, shown in **Figure 1**, takes into account the financial aspects (left brain) of a company plus creative insights (right brain) with respect to culture and emotions. By combining the two, managers should have an edge for providing value-added returns for clients. This presentation focuses on using whole brain analysis (quantitative and qualitative assessments) to determine the quality of a company's earnings and its management.

Quality of Earnings

Wall Street is preoccupied with left-brain measurements such as quarterly results and earnings surprises relative to consensus, often to the point of ignoring the quality of earnings almost entirely. The real surprises might well be no earnings increases at all. A reported earnings increase might actually be accounting driven—that is, purely a function of

changes in accounting rather than changes in the real earnings of the company. Similarly, items that are declared "somewhat" unusual are real, use cash, and lower the quality of earnings. Therefore, we need to find the reality in reported earnings. The following examples illustrate such opportunities.

Surprise and Consensus. Although most companies tend to exaggerate earnings, some actually "lowball" their earnings. If a company is marking down its earnings to save something for tomorrow, that savings will be a pleasant earnings surprise later. For example, Albertson's opened or remodeled about 100 grocery stores in 1997 and amortized the costs equally over all four quarters. But most of the stores actually opened in the second half of the year; the company thus underestimated or understated to some degree its earnings in the first half. An analyst sensitive to this subtle accounting approach would be better positioned to seize an opportunity if the stock were to weaken because of this understatement of earnings.

Some companies still believe in paying less taxes (it is part of their culture), which, of course, results in lower reported earnings. Typical methods of achieving this result include using a shorter life for depreciation, expensing items that could be capitalized, and simply using conservative accounting practices. Knowing that a company follows these practices is important when assessing the quality of earnings.

"Normal" Unusual Accounting Items. Analysts should routinely examine the "normal" unusual accounting items: reserves, gains/losses, LIFO, FIFO,

Figure 1. Whole Brain Analysis

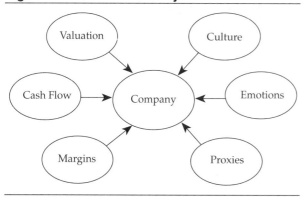

tax rates, and share repurchases. Two items that are often ignored by analysts may prove to be worth more attention: working capital management and allowance for doubtful accounts.

Working capital management is becoming increasingly important as companies search for better margins. For example, American Greetings Corporation has recently been managing its working capital much better than in the past. The resulting improvement in its cash flow has resulted in lower debt and interest expense, increased share repurchases, and incremental earnings for the company. Analysts alert to this trend may have seized an opportunity for their clients.

In today's economic environment, companies should raise their allowances for doubtful accounts. Unfortunately, doing so causes higher expenses and lower margins. For many retailers, delinquencies and bankruptcies are rising, are less predictable, and need to be monitored more carefully than in the past. Analysts should note companies that are not raising their allowances for doubtful accounts, because those companies may experience a negative surprise later.

Restructuring. Restructuring charges are becoming larger and more frequent than in the past, with companies writing off billions of dollars in restructuring costs each year. Analysts must determine the nature of these charges and their impact on profits and cash flows. As a result of restructuring, a company can suddenly show higher margins and a higher return on capital; investors must not be misled. Is the restructuring charge related to severance payments? Did the company's earnings increase exclusively because the depreciation expense went down as a result of the write-off of assets? The latter type of earnings increase is low quality and should not be accorded full credit. This restructuring activity and accounting for it increases the need for careful cash flow analysis.

Research and Development. Companies have some discretion as to whether to capitalize or expense certain R&D costs, and they can make this decision without being explicit. For example, one company had $25 million in aggregate R&D spending in 1996 and 1997. In 1996, the company expensed $15 million and capitalized $10 million, but in 1997, the company expensed $5 million and capitalized $20 million without explicitly declaring this change in accounting. This shift is subtle but important because it increased earnings by 10 cents per share at this company—without changing the level of R&D spending.

Pension and Investment Accounting. Management's choice of a discount rate and investment rate for the company's pension plan has a big impact on earnings. When interest rates fluctuate, management's decision to change the discount rate will have an impact on both liabilities and expenses. Analysts should watch for the impact from period to period. Likewise, a change in the investment rate assumption is also important. For example, NCR Corporation recently raised its assumed rate of return for the pension plan from 9 percent to 9.5 percent, which resulted in an 11 cent EPS increase. How much should investors pay for those earnings?

Similarly, a change in the investment assumptions for company-owned life insurance (COLI) has an immediate impact on the income statement and could have another, more subtle, impact later. The immediate impact is that the selling, general, and administrative expenses go up with a corresponding decrease in taxes; the company's EPS figure is unaffected, but the margin composition is certainly altered. At a later date, gains or losses from the invested funds related to this COLI may be realized and included in "other income." Recently, Albertson's reported such a gain to the tune of 10 cents per share. Again, how much should investors pay for that earnings increment?

Acquisitions. Accounting for acquisitions involves a number of issues that analysts need to pay attention to, such as the difference between pooling and purchase methods. A major acquisition-related issue is the objectivity of *pro forma* statements, which are the company's restated numbers to what they would have been had the company made certain decisions and assumptions. These *pro forma* statements allow for some creativity that analysts must be alert to when measuring the company's progress with these data.

Another area of concern is accounting for an "additive" acquisition. Leggett & Platt made an acquisition in 1996, wrote off plant and equipment, and had a special charge for compensation and debt retirement—many of these items were cash—to the tune of 30 cents per share. The company referred to these as nonrecurring items; the stock rose. Watson Pharmaceuticals made an acquisition, wrote off the acquisition costs, and reported an EPS of 56 cents. Had Watson Pharmaceuticals included the acquisition costs, its EPS would have been 43 cents—essentially flat from the previous period. Nevertheless, Wall Street chose to ignore the poor quality of earnings and took the stock up more than 20 percent.

Summary. Analysts and accountants do not necessarily have an adversarial relationship; however, some accounting policies certainly give cause to reflect and ponder the earnings being reported. If, in the short run, a momentum market ignores the quality of earnings, the alert analyst may have a unique investment opportunity.

Quality of Management

Opportunities abound for creative analysis of the quality of a company's management. When evaluating a company's prospects, analysts need to look beyond the numbers and focus on the company's culture and the emotional factors, which subsequently affect the company's stock value. Part of the purpose of this process is to determine the risk tolerance of the board and management and anticipate the risk they will assume or avert in pursuit of their corporate goals. The company's risk tolerance, in turn, should ultimately help in assessing whether or not this company's stock is a good match for your clients' risk tolerances and your particular investment approach. Two good resources exist for conducting this type of right-brain analysis: proxies and conference calls.

Proxies. The proxy, which is too often overlooked, is a terrific source of insight into a company's culture. Money managers need to read proxies and vote them; it is part of their responsibility to clients. Companies have cultures, cultures influence outcomes, and cultures change slowly; therefore, understanding a company's culture is an important part of the process of making good investment judgments. Proxies provide important insights into management, the compensation system, party of interest transactions, and ownership.

■ *Management and directors.* The proxy tells who the players are, their backgrounds, and their relationships. Are there interlocking directorships? Do many of the directors have the same last name (i.e., are they related)? A family-influenced company might be less vulnerable or receptive to the Street's pressures, and the family might take a long-term

view of running the company. This kind of culture may be good or bad for investors, so what is important is to explicitly make the determination of the kind of culture in place at the company.

The old saying "birds of a feather flock together" can help when looking at a company. Having someone from Company A (a well-respected and well-managed company) join the board of Company B is generally positive for Company B. Normally, top-quality people do not waste their time on the boards of second-rate companies, given the responsibility and liability involved. Conversely, having a top manager from a second-rate firm join the board of Company B is discouraging.

Analyzing board composition also reveals likely sources of internal pressure. Finding the source of power and pressure is a great discovery. For example, Dayton Hudson Corporation has three retail divisions, one of which has been a serious underperformer. Pressure has been exerted by the Street to fix the division, sell it, or spin it off. Dayton Hudson's board of directors includes three CEOs of companies that have been through, or are going through, a similar process. These board members are likely saying, "Let's get on with this. We have gone through it. Our shareholders will be better off." Their influence and experience create a positive environment for change.

Another example is Waste Management, which has had poor earnings for several years and is viewed as having a weak board of directors. Recently, however, several of the directors were replaced in concert with the hiring of a bold and charismatic chair. Perhaps this culture is changing rapidly enough to create an attractive investment opportunity while the Street remains emotionally negative on the company.

■ *Compensation system.* The way a company handles management compensation and incentives, both of which are disclosed in the proxy, can provide insight about its culture. Do the members of the board of directors receive perks? Are they offered benefits, including pension funds? Do they have stock options, and what are the terms of those options? Is the company simply giving them stock? How deep do the stock options go into lower management? The motivation of the board of directors and management should resemble clients' motivation—profitability and a higher stock price. Employment contracts are also worth reading about in the proxy. Is the CEO financially better off working or terminated? The incentive systems for managers and directors speaks volumes about a company's culture.

■ *Party of interest transactions.* The existence and nature of these items can be very revealing. For example, a family-controlled cruise company also owns the primary travel agency that books its trips.

How much pressure is the company putting on this travel agency to keep commissions down? This arrangement is not necessarily bad, but it is clearly important to be aware that it exists.

■ *Ownership.* Knowing who owns a company's stock provides useful information. Not all investors have the same objectives and behavior. Are the stockholders a control factor or passive investors? Stylistic investors—value, growth, momentum, and "black box"—respond differently to events. Understanding and knowing who owns the stock is an important perspective for anticipating the responses of the owners and the resulting impact on the stock price. If a company's stock is owned by investors with a wide variety of investment styles, the company may be going through a transition from growth to value, or vice versa. Information on who owns a stock can be found in the proxy, in the 13F filings with the SEC, and through various commercial services that show ownership and changes in ownership on a quarterly basis.

Conference Calls. Discovering the mindset of management and investors provides insight, particularly when a company is at a turning point, positive or negative. Analysts who know the company's management well will have a better chance to detect these emotions. Conference calls are a terrific way to observe emotions in action. The nature of the questions being asked and the nature of management's response can be good clues to the underlying emotions. Listen to the tone of the call; go beyond the numbers. Is the emotion negative, positive, timid, frustrated, defensive, or exuberant? Emotional indicators have the greatest value at the extremes, and the investment management business tends to cluster at the extremes. For example, investors have a tendency to relate the price level of the stock to the quality of management. Several years ago, Lee Iacocca, then CEO of Chrysler Corporation, commented, "When Chrysler's stock was $3 a share, I was considered inept, but when it was $47, all of a sudden I was a genius." Overcoming the emotional mindset of the Street and being able to detect this "switch point" can be extremely helpful and profitable.

Sell-side analysts are something of an intermediary among management, investors, the sales force, and the trading desk. This vicarious position makes sell-side analysts some of the most emotional players in the business. As a result, their opinions and estimates can be extrapolations of a trend and overrun reality. Be sensitive to this fact and avoid the extremes.

Another emotion to watch for is analysts' preoccupation with their own estimates, rather than how the company is doing relative to its history and its peers. What is being measured—the analyst's forecasting skills or the company's progress? The latter is what will eventually be important, and portfolio managers need to be alert to this emotional view and invest around it, rather than be biased by it.

Another factor to look for is other analysts' *and* our own biases regarding where we want a stock to go. Many times, we miss buy or sell opportunities and hope the stock will give us a second chance. During such a period, we may consciously or unconsciously allow our opinions and the tone of our reports to be biased by this desire, regardless of whether or not reality has turned against and without us. Be alert to this emotional bias.

Conclusion

In the final analysis, the quality of earnings and management will determine the valuation of a company's stock. Although many approaches exist for analyzing a company, using whole brain analysis—of earnings and management, of culture and emotions—can provide extra insight, extra focus, and an extra return to investors who can master perspective and patience. The ultimate measure of this mastery is the client's willingness to stay with a money manager during those inevitable periods when the manager's disciplined approach is temporarily out of phase.

Question and Answer Session

Fred H. Speece, CFA

Question: How important are write-offs in a forward-looking valuation model?

Speece: This is an important part of the analytical process and is becoming even more important as write-offs and restructuring become more prevalent. It is not practical to adjust future earnings and cash flow models for these write-offs; therefore, analysts are forced to accept them as one-time charges. The simplest adjustment is to change the discount rate to reflect the lower quality of future earnings resulting from the write-offs. Although this is a simple solution, many analysts do not make this adjustment and their expected returns are overstated. Another approach is to focus more on cash flow analysis than earnings.

Question: How important is the quality of earnings, if most of Wall Street simply focuses on whether earnings are going up or down?

Speece: For several years, liquidity and sheer momentum have led the way; clearly, earnings quality has not been the focus. When the momentum slows, and it will, quality earnings will prevail.

It is sometimes frustrating being disciplined, but you must be. The ultimate test is your client. What does your client expect from you? What is your role? Are you the momentum or the value manager? Give them what you promised and what they expect.

Question: How do you view estimates of merger synergies?

Speece: Frankly, such estimates are management's best guess. The answer, then, lies with the degree of confidence you have in their ability to guess and be candid with you. Is this synergy number something they can achieve, or is it a number to justify the high price the company paid?

Question: What level of inside ownership do you consider optimal?

Speece: We like to see 20–25 percent insider ownership because it clearly puts management on the same path as our clients. This level generally reduces the involvement of the extremely large institutional investors and the brokerage firms that will cover the company. Although reducing this involvement can create some inefficiency

in pricing of the stock, it does provide a valuable opportunity for our clients.

Question: How do you view companies whose growth is primarily driven by acquisition rather than internal growth?

Speece: The answer depends on the situation and investors' expectations. For example, Leggett & Platt has a history of growing through acquisitions, and its investors expect growth to come in the form of well-conceived and well-executed acquisitions.

Question: Please address the problem of a company announcing a stock repurchase versus actually repurchasing that stock.

Speece: The problem is one of follow-through. When a company announces a share repurchase, the market typically gets excited. Presumably, the company is sending a signal that it believes the stock is undervalued. If a company does not follow through, this inevitably will be a disappointment and hurt the credibility of management and the stock valuation.

Traditional Equity Valuation Methods

Thomas A. Martin, Jr., CFA
Portfolio Manager
INVESCO Capital Management, Incorporated

Traditional equity valuation methods are simply ways of exercising the critical judgment needed to determine value between the extremes of "cheap" and "expensive." Whether used for screening purposes or for fundamental analysis, such methods allow investors to make rational and consistent assessments of potential changes in key valuation inputs.

Valuation is all about judgment. At the extremes of cheap or expensive, value is obvious, but between those extremes, analysis and judgment are crucial for determining value. Traditional equity valuation methods are simply ways of performing analysis and exercising judgment. None of these methods consistently works particularly better than any of the others, and to a certain degree, they tend to give similar buy/sell signals for specific stocks. Still, these traditional methods are useful for thinking about stocks and what should drive buying and selling decisions.

Although the traditional valuation methods are relatively simple, their compelling advantage is that analysts understand what these methods are indicating. Most of the time when an analyst or a portfolio manager talks about valuation, stock selection, or the investment process, the decision ultimately comes down to picking cheap stocks. Stocks are considered cheap on some basis. When that basis is not something complex and sophisticated—such as franchise value or firm value or economic value added or some measure of cash flow that is "not distorted by accounting measures"—the traditional methods, which are, in turn, based on accounting measures, are pretty much all that is left. Even some of the newer approaches fall back ultimately on traditional measures. Thus, traditional valuation measures should be well understood by all analysts.

The goal of this presentation is to remind equity analysts of the nature of these traditional methods—how they work, their effective use, and their limitations. The presentation begins by considering the purpose of valuation. It then goes on to define traditional valuation methods and looks at how they are used for screening and in fundamental equity analysis and valuation.

Purpose

Analysts all want to buy stocks that will go up and sell stocks that will go down. A stock goes up or down from its current level because of some fundamental reevaluation of the company and its prospects or of the environment in which the company operates. This fundamental reevaluation comes about either because something has changed or is perceived to have changed in the world. Probably no model can predict actual or perceived changes in a direct and explicit way, but the models that seem to work the best do so because, for whatever reason, they capture those changes. Traditional equity valuation methods, and fundamental analysis in general, try to get at the nature of those changes.

Various factors affect a firm's value. Certainly, environmental influences—such as inflation, taxes, and available rates of return on a variety of assets—affect all companies and all valuations. Those influences are valuation inputs because they affect companies at the macro level. Company-specific influences, such as the current earnings and the future growth of those earnings, also affect valuation. In fact, at its simplest, value is the consistent piling up of profits. In addition, the level and trend of a company's risk, as well as that of the environment, affects the company's valuation; assessing risk is probably the most difficult and least effectively accomplished of all the equity analyst's tasks.

Therefore, the process of seeking buy opportunities involves identifying those companies for which the current expectations built into the current price are likely to be less than what will actually happen. Thus, the analyst needs models that will help identify (1) companies for which consensus future expected earnings are less than what "true" earnings will be or

(2) companies for which the consensus expected risk is higher than what the "true" risk will be.

Shortcuts

How are analysts to solve the daunting problem of determining which companies and stocks have value? So much data and information are available. The world is very complicated, and shortcuts are not only helpful but also nearly mandatory. These shortcuts can be categorized into two groups: expectational models and valuation models.

Expectational Models. The focus in expectational models is typically the so-called momentum measures: earnings surprise, earnings revisions, or other technical measures. These models assume that the trend that is in place will stay in place. In the case of earnings surprise, for instance, it is not the existence of the last earnings surprise that will provide outperformance. Rather, it is the fact that the last earnings surprise is a good predictor that another earnings surprise will occur. By definition, nobody expects that next earning surprise because the market efficiently adjusts its expectations. But much of the time, expectations are not adjusted enough. So, in an expectational model, a company keeps reporting positive earnings surprises, and the analysts keep raising earnings estimates until the company hits the wall and announces significantly disappointing news. Then, all the expectation-oriented investors sell the stock, and the stock's price goes down some large percentage in one day.

Valuation Models. Valuation models are typically based on mean-reversion, or contrarian, approaches. They assume that the trend that is in place will reverse and revert to some mean value. For example, suppose a company reports a big disappointment in earnings because of a sales shortfall and margin contraction. The sales shortfall and margin contraction result from some combination of short- and long-term factors. Earnings estimates are cut, and the stock price is hammered. The price may go down so much that the stock becomes cheap relative to traditional benchmarks. Mean reversion suggests that the stock price has overreacted, earnings expectations are now too low, and in the longer-term, the company will recover.

Traditional Valuation Methods

Despite their differences, both expectational and valuation models are ultimately trying to do the same thing: Identify those companies for which the current expectations built into today's stock price are wrong. Traditional equity valuation models and methods are

simply systematic ways of trying to make that identification.

The four primary traditional methods for equity valuation use the price-to-book ratio (P/B), price-to-sales ratio (P/S), price-to-earnings ratio (P/E), and the dividend discount model (DDM).

P/B. Book value is a static historical measure that does not take into account the going-concern value of a firm. Book value is calculated in relation to assets, not to the ability to generate profits. The P/B does not explicitly or even implicitly account for growth or risk of a company, and it is subject to a substantial amount of accounting measurement error because book value accumulates on the balance sheet. Management can make accounting choices in terms of timing, inventories, depreciation, write-offs, write-downs, capitalization versus expensing, and how many shares the company repurchases and at what price. Then there are intangibles. If intangibles—brands, patents, relationships, employees, technology, know-how, and so on—make up a substantial portion of a company's assets, the company will show a low book value relative to "reality."

If book value presents problems in its use, one might question the logic of using it. P/B is useful, however, for valuing (1) asset-rich companies, (2) non-going-concern situations, and (3) mature or cyclical companies with essentially zero or negative earnings. In the case of the latter, P/B, along with historical and expected return on equity (ROE), can help to estimate normalized peak earnings and normalized earnings ranges. In other words, using P/B can provide guidance when a company does not have any earnings or when earnings do not seem to be the immediate value driver. P/B can also be used to help differentiate among companies within a homogenous industry.

P/S. Like P/B, P/S does not explicitly account for the growth or risk of a company. Sometimes P/S is viewed favorably because it is the least subject to accounting manipulations of all the traditional valuation measures. At the same time, P/S is also the number with the least amount of embedded information: It is a long way from the sales line on the income statement to the EPS line, and certainly, a lot of value is made or lost as we go from one to the other. P/S may not be subject to manipulation, but a lot of crucial information is left out.

P/S can be used in the same ways as P/B. For a mature or cyclical company with essentially zero or negative earnings, P/S in conjunction with margin assumptions can identify normalized levels for the next peak earnings or normalized earnings. P/S can be helpful for evaluating companies with large recurring revenue bases or companies with high levels of intangibles. As with P/B, P/S can be used to help differentiate among companies in a homogenous industry.

P/E. The problem with P/E, like P/S and P/B, is that it does not explicitly account for growth or risk. In addition, P/E is difficult to put into perspective when EPS is declining or negative because of cyclicality or distress or when the company is in the early stages of its life cycle. But P/E is probably the most commonly used valuation measure, and analysts all know what it means to say that a company is cheap on a P/E basis. P/E is most effectively used to evaluate and compare stable companies in the late growth and maturity stages of their life cycles.

DDM. The DDM is intellectually and ideally the best model for valuing companies. The generalized formula is next year's dividend divided by some discount rate that is appropriate for that year, plus the second year's dividend divided by some discount rate that is appropriate for that year, and so on. The generalized model requires the analyst to estimate a dividend for every year from now to eternity as well as the appropriate discount rate, which may be different from year to year because inflation, the expected return on alternative investments, and the risk of the company and of the market itself may all be different from year to year. For the constant-growth version, the DDM states that a company's stock price is equal to the next year's dividend divided by the difference between k, the required rate of return, and g, the expected dividend growth rate in perpetuity. The DDM also comes in multistage models, which can vary from 2-stage models to 102-stage models. Multistage DDMs usually have a supernormal period in which earnings growth or dividend growth is higher than the long-term average for a mature company. Then they have a normalization period, during which the dividend growth rate reverts to some long-term sustainable level, and finally, a mature period, in which the dividend growth rate is constant.

An advantage of any DDM approach is that all of the input assumptions can be as explicit, complicated, and specific as the analyst desires. Building such a model forces the analyst to ask important questions: What does this company do? What products does it make? What stage of its industry, company, and product life cycle is the company in, in terms of its sales, profitability, and returns? The DDM makes the analyst think about these factors and put them in the model explicitly, whereas the other traditional models do not. The drawback is that the analyst has to make many assumptions, and there are a lot of places to go wrong. Small changes in key assumptions, especially in the growth rate and the discount rate, can have a big effect on the valuation estimate generated by the model.

Screening

The first potential use for these traditional valuation methods is to look for ways of narrowing the overwhelmingly large universe of investable companies down to some number of reasonable candidates that are more likely to have the desired value characteristics. This process is called screening.

Numerous studies have been done on all of the traditional valuation models, with a variety of results. Researchers contend that if portfolio managers would only follow a particular valuation model, such as low P/E, P/S, or P/B, they would be rewarded with outperformance. In fact, studies have shown that applying any one of these methods blindly and faithfully will generate outperformance over time; however, many practical reasons can be found for not applying these methods blindly and faithfully. Perhaps the most important is that such quantitatively generated portfolios typically exhibit other characteristics that may not be prudent for most investors. So, although screening is useful for identifying potential investment candidates, analysts must take care to understand the implications of the screening factor for portfolio construction.

To illustrate the biases of the traditional valuation methods, I put about 1,000 of the largest companies in the United States through five valuation screens: P/B, P/S, P/E, P/E to growth (a form of P/E valuation), and the DDM. I created five model portfolios, each consisting of the 50 cheapest stocks as defined by the particular valuation method. These five portfolios could then be compared with regard to sector composition, valuation, ROE composition, growth, and finally, risk, expectations, and performance.

Sector Composition. The sector compositions of the model portfolios are shown in **Table 1**. The S&P 500 Index, provided for reference, is a well-diversified portfolio. It represents a reasonable capitalization-weighted cross-section of the U.S. economy, and it is the benchmark against which most equity managers are compared.

In contrast, the portfolio containing the 50 cheapest stocks on the basis of the P/E-to-growth ratio is 30 percent in consumer cyclicals, 26 percent in technology, and 10 percent or less in all other sectors—not a particularly well-diversified portfolio. The P/B portfolio is 54 percent in utilities, 20 percent in cyclicals, and underweighted in everything else. Staples

Table 1. Sector Composition of Model Portfolios Based on Traditional Valuation Measures, September 30, 1997

	S&P 500	P/B	P/S	P/E	P/E to Growth	DDM
Basic materials	5%	4%	2%	8%	10%	8%
Capital goods	9	4	8	4	8	2
Communications services	6	2	0	0	0	0
Consumer cyclicals	9	20	30	16	30	18
Consumer staples	14	6	32	4	8	14
Energy	9	0	6	2	2	0
Financials	17	4	2	16	10	14
Health care	11	4	4	0	6	22
Technology	15	2	6	6	26	20
Transportation	1	0	4	0	0	0
Utilities	3	54	6	44	0	2
Total	100%	100%	100%	100%	100%	100%

▨ = Two largest overweightings in each portfolio.

☐ = Two smallest underweightings in each portfolio.

are cheap in the P/S strategy, as indicated by their overweighting, but they are not cheap by any other measure. The P/E and P/B portfolios turn out to be very similar: both overweighted in utilities and consumer cyclicals. The P/E portfolio is the only one that shows financials to be cheap. The P/E-to-growth portfolio is a reasonably well-diversified portfolio but contains no utilities. The DDM portfolio is one of the best diversified of all of the model portfolios, but it does have some overweights that seem to allow the manager to buy stocks with good growth characteristics, such as technology and health care.

The point is that most managers would not be comfortable with any of these individual portfolios, and they would have difficulty adhering to the discipline of using just one strategy no matter what type of portfolio was indicated. As an alternative, a manager might consider picking the cheapest stocks in each sector and then using the S&P 500 weights, but then that manager has diverged from the path of using a pure quantitative valuation strategy to that of using some degree of judgment. How many more good judgments will that manager have to make when the quantitative indications are not to his or her liking? The important issue, however, is that judgments *should* be made; taking a closer look at these blindly constructed portfolios reveals why judgment

is a key ingredient in valuation analysis and portfolio construction.

Valuation. The model portfolios exhibit substantially different valuations; **Table 2** shows average levels of the different valuation measures for each portfolio. The DDM portfolio is the most expensive overall; it has the highest P/E, P/S, and P/B, the next-to-lowest dividend yield, and a middle-of-the-pack P/E-to-growth value. The P/E and P/B portfolios look most like traditional value portfolios (cheap across the board). The P/E-to-Growth column, however, shows something very interesting: Investors are paying a very high price for each unit of growth in those P/B and P/E portfolios, which is important because, as mentioned earlier, growth is a factor not explicitly accounted for in these models.

ROE Composition. The average operating characteristics of the portfolios constructed from the traditional valuation methods are shown in **Table 3**. For example, no one should be surprised that the DDM portfolio is composed of higher-ROE companies, which are driven by high margins and relatively high leverage. Similarly, the P/B portfolio has the lowest ROE, which is a function of low turnover and relatively low leverage. The P/S portfolio has the highest

Table 2. Average Valuation Measures of Model Portfolios, September 30, 1997

Portfolio	P/E	Dividend Yield	P/S	P/B	P/E to Growth
DDM	18.1	1.1%	3.4	4.0	1.6
P/B	11.9	4.2	0.9	1.1	3.4
P/S	14.2	1.7	0.3	1.7	1.6
P/E	10.2	4.3	1.0	1.4	2.5
P/E to growth	13.5	0.8	1.9	2.4	0.7

Table 3. ROE Composition of Model Portfolios, September 30, 1997

| Portfolio | 5-Year Average ROE | Total Debt[a] | | Asset Turnover | | Operating Margin | |
		Current	5-Year Average	Last 12 Months	5-Year Average	Current	5-Year Average
DDM	30.5%	213.9%	172.3%	1.1	1.2	24.3%	24.8%
P/B	9.6	101.8	99.1	0.9	0.9	15.1	16.2
P/S	11.8	95.1	87.2	2.7	2.6	3.7	4.3
P/E	12.2	177.6	172.8	0.9	0.9	19.5	19.5
P/E to growth	13.4	77.6	74.9	1.4	1.4	14.2	12.6

[a]Total debt as a percentage of total equity.

asset turnover but the lowest margins, which means that these companies have fairly high operating leverage. The P/E-to-growth portfolio is the only portfolio that has companies with expanding margins.

Table 3 raises interesting questions about the operating characteristics of the companies in each of the portfolios and the biases of the traditional valuation measures. Why are these companies cheap? Where are they in their business cycles and product cycles? What are the implications for future stability, growth, and risk? For example, for the P/E-to-growth companies, is the growth coming only from expanding margins, or are these companies achieving unit growth as well? Are these companies cheap because the market does not want to pay for margin expansion but would rather pay for unit growth? Perhaps margin expansion is sustainable in the case of one company but not another. Perhaps it is a more sustainable source of growth for one company than continued unit growth is for another. Further analysis to answer these questions will lead to a better understanding of the fundamental risks being assumed when investing in specific companies.

Growth. The growth characteristics of the five model portfolios are shown in **Table 4**. Across the board, the DDM portfolio's 10-year growth measures are the best of any of these portfolios. Does that mean that those growth rates are sustainable going forward? Not necessarily; this result could be an artifact of the method of constructing the model. To construct this DDM, I used the past 10 years of history as a prediction for the normalized values going forward. So, the fact that the DDM portfolio has the highest growth measures is not much of a coincidence. This finding certainly argues for care in assessing model inputs and the biases imparted by those inputs.

Other model biases also show up in these portfolios. The P/B portfolio has the highest book value growth in the past year; sales growth in the P/S model portfolio has been the highest in the past year versus all of the other portfolios; and the P/E-to-growth portfolio has the best recent and forecasted EPS growth. The P/E portfolio generally exhibits the

lowest growth record across the board. Because the market is forward looking, perhaps these companies are not cheap at all but are properly priced relative to low expected growth. On the other hand, maybe the growth expectations are too low because of incorrect extrapolation of the past. Thus, Table 4 points out two important considerations: (1) the need to recognize that the valuation model used, by definition, will yield certain biases and (2) the need for further company-specific research to understand these companies' potential risks and returns.

Risk, Expectations, and Performance. The portfolios' risk levels, expectations, and performance characteristics are shown in **Table 5**. The P/E and P/B portfolios have the lowest betas and the lowest tracking errors (R^2) with the S&P 500, but they also have exhibited the worst earnings trends relative to current expectations. For the Earnings Surprise Rank and the Earnings Estimate Trend Rank columns, 100 is considered poor and 1 is good. If the P/E and P/B portfolios had values of 1 for those columns, they would be reporting huge positive surprises and estimates would be going up. So, the P/E and P/B portfolios have poor earnings trends. In addition, the stocks in the P/E and P/B portfolios are "down and out," especially when viewed by their three-year and one-year performance numbers, although they started to make a slight comeback in the past three months. The P/S portfolio is again in the middle. It has a beta of 1.03, has low tracking with the S&P 500 (0.55), and is neutral on earnings and expectations. The P/E-to-growth portfolio has the highest beta of all the portfolios, probably driven by its technology exposure, but it still has a low R^2. Also, the stocks in this portfolio have gone up the most in the past one-year and three-year periods. The DDM portfolio is a conservative portfolio, which is reflected in its performance characteristics.

Tables 1 through 5 illustrate a crucial point: Each of the traditional valuation measures biases stock selection in many different ways—from growth history and prospects to operating characteristics, to recently reported results and stock performance, to

Table 4. Growth Characteristics of Model Portfolios, September 30, 1997
(percents)

Portfolio	Primary EPS Growth		I/B/E/S Estimated EPS			Sustainable Growth			Sales per Share Growth			Book Value per Share Growth		
	5 Years	10 Years	FY1-Actual Percent Change	FY2-FY1 Percent Change	Next 5 Years Forecast Growth	1 Year	5 Years	10 Years	1 Year	5 Years	10 Years	1 Year	5 Years	10 Years
DDM	20.1	21.2	13.4	14.0	15.7	19.8	20.4	22.2	14.3	17.2	17.8	10.9	19.4	20.8
P/B	6.0	1.2	176.4	20.5	7.2	3.6	-1.7	0.0	7.4	4.1	4.7	24.7	5.4	6.2
P/S	6.3	4.6	15.9	29.2	12.9	7.0	6.2	6.6	17.0	10.8	10.4	15.7	8.6	9.3
P/E	12.3	3.1	2.6	14.6	8.1	4.8	0.1	1.3	6.6	3.6	5.0	21.3	5.8	5.1
P/E to growth	33.5	13.9	23.9	33.2	21.2	14.5	11.0	11.2	14.5	12.3	12.5	11.6	15.5	13.5

FY = fiscal year.

Table 5. Risk, Expectations, and Performance Characteristics of Model Portfolios, September 30, 1997

Portfolio	Portfolio Beta	R^2	Earnings Surprise Rank	Earnings Estimate Trend Rank	Price Change Relative to S&P 500		
					3 Months	52 Weeks	3 Years
DDM	1.11	0.86	52	49	0.60%	0.07%	8.12%
P/B	0.59	0.48	65	64	2.87	−15.65	−42.11
P/S	1.03	0.55	53	56	7.11	−2.14	−27.70
P/E	0.63	0.53	64	63	1.92	−17.15	−31.18
P/E to growth	1.22	0.57	57	64	−0.62	2.44	28.77

degree of diversification. Analysts and portfolio managers must recognize these biases, understand their implications, and use the information as a guide for further research and insight into specific company risks and returns.

Fundamental Analysis

In addition to screening the universe of stocks into a more manageable set, traditional valuation methods can be used to look for insights into how a company is priced in the market relative to its factual, historical record and relative to any predictions about its future economic performance. This process is typically called fundamental analysis, and the DDM is an often-used application in this context.

Growth and Discount Rates. A two-stage DDM can be used to isolate the valuation impact of growth and discount rates. For simplicity, assume that the first stage runs for 10 years and that the company has growth in excess of the mature growth rate for that 10-year period. The second stage is the mature stage; assume that the company will grow at

the average long-term historical earnings growth rate of the S&P 500 from Year 11 through eternity. This framework allows an analyst to pose some interesting questions regarding the growth and discount rates that are embedded in an observed stock price.

Suppose, for instance, that the two-stage DDM is applied to the stock of Microsoft Corporation and International Paper (IP). On September 30, 1997, as shown in **Table 6**, Microsoft's stock price was $132.31 and IP's stock price was $55.00. With second-stage growth constant at 6.50 percent annually (which is the S&P 400 Industrials long-term growth rate) for both companies and first-stage annual growth estimates generated by Wall Street of 23.80 percent for Microsoft and 16.20 percent for IP, the respective prices would be $132.58 and $33.90. With a constant discount rate for each company, the DDM framework allows an analyst to solve for the first-stage growth rate implied by any stock price. For example, Microsoft's September 30, 1997, stock price implies a first-stage growth rate of 23.78 percent, only 2 basis points (bps) off the Wall Street estimate. By contrast,

Table 6. First-Stage Implied Growth Rate Comparisons: Microsoft and International Paper

Item	Microsoft	International Paper
Price as of 9/30/97	$132.31	$55.00
Price implied by current estimate	132.58	33.90
Current estimates		
Second-stage growth assumptions[a]	6.50%	6.50%
First-stage growth assumptions[b]	23.80	16.20
First-stage growth rate implied by current price	23.78	22.67
Percent of value in first stage	0.00	25.92
First-stage growth rate implied by one-half current price	15.49	13.44
Percent of value in first stage	0.00	32.22
First-stage growth rate implied by twice the current price	32.66	32.25
Percent of value in first stage	0.00	21.42

Note: First-stage discount rate = Beta × Risk premium + Risk-free rate = Stock's current beta × 3 + 6.5.
Second-stage discount rate = Beta × Risk premium + Risk-free rate = Stock beta of 1 × 3 + 6.5.

[a]Based on long-term growth rate of S&P 400 Industrials for the 1963–96 period.
[b]I/B/E/S mean five-year future growth estimate.

IP's September 30, 1997, stock price implies a first-stage growth rate of 22.67 percent, contrasted to the Street's 16.20 percent growth estimate. Is IP overpriced? Will it be able to grow for the next 10 years at a rate nearly 650 bps higher than analysts are expecting? At this point, judgment about the model comes in. What would it take to cut the stock price in half? What growth rate would be implied? If Microsoft grew at only 15.5 percent, the stock should fall by about half. If IP grew at only 13 percent on average for 10 years, the stock price would be cut in half. Could the two stock prices double? Holding everything else constant, both companies would have to grow at a rate higher than 32 percent for the next 10 years for the two prices to double. Finally, this analysis shows that none of Microsoft's value is explicitly derived from first-stage growth because of the assumption that Microsoft does not pay a dividend at all in the first stage; however, roughly 20–30 percent of IP's value is first-stage based, depending on which measure is examined.

Table 7 shows exactly the same analysis with only one change: The first-stage growth rates are held constant at the levels estimated by Wall Street, and the second-stage growth necessary to generate specific stock prices is identified. Again, Microsoft is priced as though it will grow at a rate close to that second-stage growth rate, as was the case in Table 6. IP has to grow at a much higher growth rate than Microsoft (7.89 percent versus 6.49 percent) to justify the current stock price. A growth rate of 7.89 percent may not seem high, but this is the second-stage

(infinite) growth rate, and 7.89 percent is a high sustainable growth rate for infinity. For these two companies' stock prices to be cut in half, Microsoft would have to grow at 3.65 percent and IP at 5.43 percent. For their stock prices to double, Microsoft would have to grow forever at a rate that is almost 1.5 percent, and IP almost 2.5 percent, above the long-term growth rate of the economy.

The same analytical approach can be applied to solving for implied discount rates, as shown in **Table 8** and **Table 9**. By holding the second-stage discount rate constant at 9.50 percent for both companies and solving for the first-stage discount rate implied in the given stock prices, one can see an interesting result. Table 8 shows that the first-stage discount rate is irrelevant for Microsoft, because all of the stock price is reflected in the second-stage, or terminal, value. By contrast, IP's first-stage discount rate is negative at the current or any higher stock price, indicating that the current stock price cannot be justified at any discount rate, given the growth assumptions.

In Table 9, the first-stage discount rates are held constant to solve for the implied second-stage discount rates. Again, Microsoft is priced in line with the expectations shown in this table, and IP is mispriced by almost 130 bps, as measured in the second-stage discount rate. For the stock prices to fall by half, interest rates have to rise considerably, but relatively smaller interest rate declines will allow the stock prices to double.

Table 7. Second-Stage Implied Growth Rate Comparison: Microsoft and International Paper

Item	Microsoft	International Paper
Price as of 9/30/97	$132.31	$55.00
Price implied by current estimate	132.58	33.90
Current estimates		
First-stage growth assumptions[a]	23.80%	16.20%
Second-stage growth assumptions[b]	6.50	6.50
Second-stage growth rate implied by current price	6.49	7.89
Percent of value in first stage	0.00	18.54
Second-stage growth rate implied by one-half current price	3.65	5.43
Percent of value in first stage	0.00	37.10
Second-stage growth rate implied by twice the current price	7.98	8.77
Percent of value in first stage	0.00	9.30

Note: First-stage discount rate = Beta × Risk premium + Risk-free rate = Stock's current beta × 3 + 6.5.
Second-stage discount rate = Beta × Risk premium + Risk-free rate = Stock beta of 1 × 3 + 6.5.

[a]I/B/E/S mean five-year future growth estimate.
[b]Based on long-term growth rate of S&P 400 Industrials for the 1963–96 period.

Table 8. First-Stage Implied Discount Rate Comparisons: Microsoft and International Paper

Item	Microsoft	International Paper
Price as of 9/30/97	$132.31	$55.00
Price implied by current estimate	132.58	33.90
Current estimates		
Second-stage discount rate assumptions[a]	9.50%	9.50%
First-stage discount rate assumptions[b]	10.34	9.83
First-stage discount rate implied by current price	na[c]	–7.30
Percent of value in first stage	0.00	56.92
First-stage discount rate implied by one-half current price	na[c]	32.84
Percent of value in first stage	0.00	13.83
First-stage discount rate implied by twice the current price	na[c]	–18.86
Percent of value in first stage	0.00	78.46

na = not applicable.

Note: First-stage growth rate is based on the I/B/E/S five-year future growth estimate.
Second-stage growth rate is based on long-term growth rate of S&P 400 Industrials for the 1963–96 period.

[a]Second-stage discount rate = Beta × Risk premium + Risk-free rate = Stock beta of 1 × 3 + 6.5.
[b]First-stage discount rate = Beta × Risk premium + Risk-free rate = Stock's current beta × 3 + 6.5.
[c]All value is in terminal value.

Table 9. Second-Stage Implied Discount Rate Comparisons: Microsoft and International Paper

Item	Microsoft	International Paper
Price as of 9/30/97	$132.31	$55.00
Price implied by current estimate	132.58	33.90
Current estimates		
First-stage discount rate assumptions[a]	10.34%	9.83%
Second-stage discount rate assumptions[b]	9.50	9.50
Second-stage discount rate implied by current price	9.49	8.28
Percent of value in first stage	0.00	18.59
Second-stage discount rate implied by one-half current price	11.51	13.44
Percent of value in first stage	0.00	58.64
Second-stage discount rate implied by twice the current price	8.19	7.37
Percent of value in first stage	0.00	9.30

Note: First-stage growth rate is based on the I/B/E/S five-year future growth estimate.
Second-stage growth rate is based on long-term growth rate of S&P 400 Industrials for the 1963–96 period.

[a]First-stage discount rate = Beta × Risk premium + Risk-free rate = Stock's current beta × 3 + 6.5.
[b]Second-stage discount rate = Beta × Risk premium + Risk-free rate = Stock beta of 1 × 3 + 6.5.

A similar type of analysis can be used to gain marketwide insights. The market is currently trading at a much higher multiple than it has in the past, causing observers to say the market is expensive. But other factors have changed from the past as well. In the past 10 years, ROEs have increased and payout ratios have decreased, so companies' sustainable growth rates have ostensibly increased. At the same time, inflation has declined, which has caused a decline in discount rates.

These changes might lead analysts to believe that different growth and discount rates affect the mar-ket's P/Es, as shown in **Table 10**. This example uses a two-stage DDM to generate the P/Es. Table 10 shows that P/Es get higher as growth rates get higher, and P/Es also get higher as discount rates get lower. Thus, one can see that P/E is exponentially, not linearly, related to growth and discount rates.

Tables 6 through 9 hinted at a key question in two-stage DDM analysis, which can be addressed by extending the perspective of Table 10: How much of the value is locked up in the first stage and how much comes from the second stage? If investors say that they want to get their money up front because it is

Table 10. P/Es as a Function of Growth and Discount Rates

Growth Rates	Discount Rates										
	5%	6%	7%	8%	9%	10%	11%	12%	13%	14%	15%
2%	9.4×	8.5×	7.7×	7.1×	6.5×	6.1×	5.7×	5.3×	5.0×	4.8×	4.5×
3%	11.0	9.9	9.0	8.2	7.6	7.1	6.6	6.2	5.8	5.6	5.3
4%	13.0	11.7	10.6	9.7	8.9	8.3	7.8	7.3	6.9	6.5	6.2
5%	15.5	13.9	12.6	11.5	10.6	9.9	9.2	8.7	8.2	7.8	7.5
6%	18.6	16.7	15.1	13.8	12.7	11.8	11.0	10.4	9.9	9.4	9.0
7%	22.5	20.1	18.2	16.6	15.3	14.3	13.4	12.6	12.0	11.4	11.0
8%	27.4	24.5	22.1	20.2	18.7	17.4	16.3	15.4	14.6	14.0	13.5
9%	33.4	29.9	27.0	24.7	22.8	21.3	20.0	18.9	18.1	17.3	16.7
10%	41.0	36.7	33.2	30.4	28.1	26.3	24.7	23.5	22.4	21.5	20.7
11%	50.5	45.2	41.0	37.6	34.8	32.6	30.7	29.2	27.9	26.9	26.0
12%	62.5	56.0	50.8	46.6	43.3	40.6	38.3	36.5	35.0	33.7	32.7
13%	77.5	69.5	63.2	58.1	54.0	50.7	48.0	45.8	44.0	42.5	41.2
14%	96.3	86.5	78.7	72.5	67.6	63.5	60.3	57.6	55.5	53.7	52.2
15%	120.0	107.9	98.4	90.8	84.7	79.8	75.9	72.7	70.1	67.9	66.1
16%	149.8	134.9	123.2	113.9	106.5	100.5	95.7	91.8	88.7	86.1	84.0
17%	187.1	168.8	154.4	143.0	133.9	126.7	120.8	116.1	112.3	109.2	106.7
18%	234.0	211.5	193.7	179.7	168.6	159.8	152.7	147.0	142.4	138.6	135.6
19%	292.9	265.1	243.3	226.1	212.5	201.7	193.0	186.1	180.5	176.0	172.3
20%	366.6	332.4	305.5	284.4	267.8	254.6	244.0	235.6	228.8	226.4	218.9
21%	459.0	416.8	383.8	357.9	337.5	321.3	308.5	298.2	290.0	283.4	278.0
22%	574.7	522.6	482.0	450.2	425.2	405.4	389.8	377.3	367.3	359.2	352.7
23%	719.3	655.1	605.2	566.1	535.5	511.3	492.2	477.0	464.8	455.1	447.2
24%	899.9	820.8	759.4	711.5	673.9	644.4	621.0	602.5	587.7	575.9	566.4

Note: Assumptions for P/E calculation: today's earnings = $1.00; constant payout ratio = 40 percent; growth is over 30 years. A constant DDM is used to calculate the terminal value with a 7 percent growth rate and a 10 percent discount rate.

less risky, then they would probably want most of their value to come from the first stage, because it is more certain than the future second stage. Using the same assumptions as in Table 10, **Table 11** shows that as either the growth rate or discount rate goes up, less and less value is created in the first stage, so risk increases as either rate increases.

Valuation. The valuation question can often be worked backward more easily than forward. In other words, determining whether a stock is cheap can be difficult, but the previous Microsoft and International Paper examples illustrated that determining the implied growth rate that justifies a company's current stock price is not so difficult.

The same logic can be applied to marketwide valuation. **Table 12** shows various valuation measures for the Nasdaq Composite Index, the S&P 500 as a whole, and the S&P 500 divided into two groups: the top 25 stocks and the bottom 475 stocks based on market capitalization. As of this analysis, the entire S&P 500 was trading at 23.7 times earnings, 3.9 times book value, and 1.6 times sales, with a dividend yield of about 1.6 percent. The two growth measures of interest are the 10-year price-implied growth (PIG) and the growth duration.

The PIG rate asks: What growth rate must this company (or group of companies in this case) sustain for the next 10 years to justify its current P/E? The PIG model simply solves for the annualized growth rate in the first stage of a two-stage DDM. In the first stage, company or index dividends are estimated using current EPS data and the current payout ratio, which is assumed to be constant. The discount rate is based on a capital asset pricing model (CAPM) framework, using a market return of 9.5 percent, a risk-free return of 6.5 percent, and the relevant company or index beta. The second stage assumes a 38 percent payout ratio, constant earnings growth of 6.5 percent, the same market and risk-free returns, and a beta of 1. The resultant 10-year PIG rate can be compared with Wall Street's 5-year expected growth rate. If the company (or group of companies) is priced so that its PIG is higher than Wall Street estimates, maybe that stock is not cheap. If it is priced so that its PIG is lower than estimates, maybe it is an attractive stock.

For instance, the S&P 500's PIG is 15.8 percent annually, but analysts say that the S&P 500 will grow at 13.8 percent annually for the next 5 years, which suggests that the S&P 500 is currently somewhat overpriced. But current "cheapness" can be assessed only in the context of the S&P 500's performance for

Table 11. First-Stage Dividend Stream as a Percentage of Total DDM Value as a Function of Growth and Discount Rates

Growth Rates	Discount Rates										
	5%	6%	7%	8%	9%	10%	11%	12%	13%	14%	15%
2%	84%	83%	81%	79%	77%	76%	74%	72%	70%	69%	67%
3%	82	80	78	76	74	72	70	68	66	64	62
4%	80	77	75	73	70	68	66	64	62	59	58
5%	77	75	72	69	67	64	62	59	57	55	53
6%	75	72	69	66	63	60	57	55	52	50	48
7%	72	69	66	63	59	56	53	51	48	46	43
8%	70	66	63	59	56	53	50	47	44	41	39
9%	68	64	60	56	53	49	46	43	40	37	35
10%	65	61	57	53	49	46	42	39	36	34	31
11%	63	59	54	50	46	43	39	36	33	30	28
12%	61	56	52	47	43	40	36	33	30	27	25
13%	59	54	49	45	41	37	33	30	27	25	22
14%	57	52	47	43	38	34	31	28	25	22	20
15%	55	50	45	40	36	32	29	26	23	20	18
16%	53	48	43	38	34	30	27	24	21	18	16
17%	51	46	41	36	32	28	25	22	19	17	15
18%	50	45	39	35	30	27	23	20	18	15	14
19%	48	43	38	33	29	25	22	19	16	14	12
20%	47	42	36	32	28	24	20	18	15	13	11
21%	46	40	35	30	26	23	19	17	14	12	10
22%	45	39	34	29	25	21	18	16	13	11	10
23%	43	38	33	28	24	20	17	15	12	11	9
24%	42	37	32	27	23	19	16	14	12	10	8

Note: Assumptions for P/E calculation: today's earnings = $1.00; constant payout ratio = 40 percent; growth is over 30 years. A constant DDM is used to calculate the terminal value with a 7 percent growth rate and a 10 percent discount rate.

long periods of time. For the past 5 years, it has grown at 18.8 percent; for the past 10 years, 12 percent; for the past 20 years, 9 percent; and for the past 30 years, 9 percent. So, will the S&P 500 grow at 15.8 percent for the next 10 years? This valuation approach allows analysts to start thinking about that question.

Growth duration measures the length of time needed to justify the spread between an individual stock's (or group of stocks') P/E and a given market-wide P/E. The growth duration formula is

$$\text{Number of years} = \frac{\ln\left(\dfrac{P/E_g}{P/E_m}\right)}{\ln\left(\dfrac{1 + G_g + D_g}{1 + G_m + D_m}\right)},$$

where

P/E_g = P/E of the growth company
P/E_m = P/E of the market
G_g = forecasted growth rate of the growth company
D_g = dividend yield of the growth company
G_m = long-term forecasted growth rate of the market
D_m = dividend yield of the market

If a company has a higher expected growth rate and a higher P/E than, for instance, the S&P 500 growth duration estimates how many years the company's earnings must grow at that expected growth rate relative to the growth rate of S&P 500 earnings to be able to justify that P/E. If the answer is many years, maybe that stock is potentially overvalued. If the answer is only a few years, maybe it is cheap.

As shown in Table 12, the Nasdaq Composite Index is about the same "price" as the S&P 500 except for its dividend yield and its P/E, which is very high—almost 75 times earnings. The Nasdaq does have a 5-year expected growth rate of 21.5 percent, but it is priced so that it has to grow at about 29 percent. It has grown at that rate for the past 5 years but not for longer periods of time. Also, the Nasdaq has to grow at the expected rate for nearly 23 years to justify its P/E versus the S&P 500.

The 5-year expected growth rate for the two S&P 500 subgroups is about the same for both, but the group composed of the top 25 market cap has a higher P/E, 25.4 versus 23.0. In fact, the top 25 group has a higher P/B, higher P/S, and lower dividend yield. For the top 25 group, the 10-year PIG rate is higher than the expected growth rate, whereas for the

Table 12. Traditional Valuation Measures for Various Indexes, September 30, 1997

Index	Trailing 12-Month Earnings P/E	P/B	P/S	Dividend Yield	5-Year Expected Growth Rate	10-Year PIG	Historical Annualized Growth Rates				Years to Justify P/E versus S&P 500 (Growth Duration)
							5 Years	10 Years	20 Years	30 Years	
Nasdaq	74.7	3.7	1.6	0.5%	21.5%	29.2%	729.8%	21.0%	17.7%	9.2%	22.7
S&P 500											
Total index	23.7	3.9	1.6	1.6	13.8	15.8	18.8	12.3	9.1	9.0	—
Top 25[a]	25.4	5.8	2.3	1.5	13.9	14.3	17.0	14.9	11.2	10.2	Never
Bottom 475[a]	23.0	3.3	1.4	1.7	13.8	12.9	20.1	10.6	7.6	8.1	–118.7

[a]Rank based on market capitalization.

bottom 475, it is lower. The bottom 475 companies have grown faster than the top 25 in the past 5 years, although they have not grown as fast for longer periods of time. In terms of the number of years to justify its P/E relative to the entire S&P 500, the top 25 group will never catch up, because its expected growth rate is essentially no higher than the S&P 500 as a whole and its P/E is much higher. The bottom 475 group is already cheaper than the entire S&P 500, which results in the negative growth duration.

Even among companies that most observers would consider to be "high flyers" are some that may be overpriced and some that may be fairly priced, as shown in **Table 13**. The companies in the overpriced group, on average, trade at 514 times the last 12 months' earnings, 19.1 times book value, and 24.3 times sales; they have no dividend yield. The 5-year expected growth rate is about 50 percent, and the 10-year PIG rate is 53.2 percent. Unfortunately, most of these companies have not been in existence long enough to have long historical records, which complicates the valuation task. The analysis does show that these companies will need 13 years at a 50 percent growth rate to justify their P/Es relative to the S&P 500.

Although many analysts say that Microsoft, PeopleSoft, and Cisco Systems are overpriced, these companies in the fairly priced group are trading at only 49 times earnings, 12.4 times book value, and 8.9 times sales, and again, they have no dividend yield. The 5-year growth rate of 32 percent is much lower than that of the overpriced stocks, but in fact, these stocks are priced as though they have to grow at only 23 percent, which is easier to imagine than 32 percent. Some of these companies do have 5- and 10-year histories. Microsoft for the past 10 years has been able to grow at 38 percent, and even for the past 5 years as a much larger company, it has been able to grow at 30 percent. Will Microsoft be able to grow at 25 percent as its PIG rate implies? Perhaps. The growth duration of this group averages 4.6 years, which suggests, for companies that are growing as fast as these, fair or even cheap pricing.

The companies in **Table 14** are those that for the past 5, 10, 20, and 30 years have had growth rates in excess of 10 percent for each of those time periods. Some of these companies are overpriced, and some are fairly priced. The group of overpriced companies has a P/E of 30.4 times; the fairly priced group has a P/E of only 18.6 times. The P/B for the overpriced group is 8.4 versus 4.1 for the fairly priced group; the P/S is 3.6 versus 1.7. The valuations are almost twice as expensive on a historical basis for the overpriced group. The expected 5-year growth rate is about the same for both groups, but the PIG rate for 10 years is much higher for the overpriced group. The historical average growth rates for the overpriced group are relatively consistent, at 13 percent, but these averages are quite a bit lower than those of the fairly priced group, for which the 10-year PIG rate is 10.9 percent and the expected 5-year growth rate is 13.5 percent. The growth durations for the companies in the overpriced group are either never (they will never be cheap) or very, very long (the average is 74 years). For the fairly priced group, the average is negative, meaning that these companies are already cheap relative to the S&P 500.

Conclusion

A valuation model is only as good as its inputs, the fundamentals that have generated those inputs, and to some degree, the history behind those fundamentals. These models generate snapshots in time. The only output that really matters is change relative to embedded assumptions. What needs to be done, then, is to use tools that reflect the underlying fundamentals and the embedded assumptions, thus allowing investors to make rational and consistent judgments about the likely direction and magnitude of change and, ultimately, to buy and sell stocks accordingly. Traditional valuation methods offer investors such a tool—one that, like all tools, has limitations, but one that is also widely applicable and relatively straightforward.

Table 13. Traditional Valuation Measures for Various High-Flyer Stocks, September 30, 1997

Ticker Symbol	Name	Trailing 12-Month Earnings P/E	P/B	P/S	Dividend Yield	5-Year Expected Growth Rate	10-Year PIG	Historical Annualized Growth Rates				Years to Justify P/E versus S&P 500 (Growth Duration)
								5 Years	10 Years	20 Years	30 Years	
Overpriced												
PCTL	PictureTel	345.8	1.4	0.8	0.0%	28.3%	51.5%	37.8%	NA	NA	NA	25.4
ABMD	Abiomed	90.8	4.4	5.9	0.0	35.0	32.5	NA	NA	NA	NA	8.6
YHOO	Yahoo	1,002.5	20.5	44.0	0.0	64.2	68.5	NA	NA	NA	NA	10.6
RMBS	Rambus	618.1	50.1	46.4	0.0	75.0	60.5	NA	NA	NA	NA	7.8
Average		514.3	19.1	24.3	0.0	50.6	53.2					13.1
Fairly Priced												
MSFT	Microsoft	49.7	15.2	14.3	0.0	23.8	24.8	30.4	38.5%	NA	NA	10.6
TLAB	Tellabs	39.0	10.6	8.5	0.0	27.4	21.8	76.7	42.5	NA	NA	5.0
PSFT	PeopleSoft	106.7	21.0	10.6	0.0	45.5	34.7	64.7	NA	NA	NA	6.5
CSCO	Cisco Systems	48.1	11.4	7.8	0.0	33.1	24.3	71.9	NA	NA	NA	5.0
INTC	Intel	23.3	8.7	6.6	0.1	21.4	15.5	42.7	35.9	28.8%	NA	0.0
ASND	Ascend	27.2	7.3	5.3	0.0	40.3	17.5	NA	NA	NA	NA	0.7
Average		49.0	12.4	8.9	0.0	31.9	23.1	57.3	39.0			4.6

NA = not available.

Table 14. Traditional Valuation Measures for Consistent Long-Term Growth Stocks, September 30, 1997

Ticker Symbol	Name	Trailing 12-Month Earnings P/E	P/B	P/S	Dividend Yield	5-Year Expected Growth Rate	10-Year PIG	Historical Annualized Growth Rates				Years to Justify P/E versus S&P 500 (Growth Duration)
								5 Years	10 Years	20 Years	30 Years	
Overpriced												
GE	General Electric	28.1	7.0	2.6	1.5%	12.9%	15.3%	13.2%	10.3%	10.6%	10.9%	Never
PBI	Pitney Bowes	24.3	5.8	3.0	1.9	13.0	13.1	11.1	12.0	11.6	12.4	Never
WAG	Walgreen	29.1	5.6	1.0	0.9	14.6	16.6	13.7	13.5	14.7	14.1	234.0
WWY	Wrigley	33.2	9.1	4.8	1.5	12.4	16.8	13.8	14.3	15.6	11.5	Never
AUD	Automatic Data	27.8	5.5	3.4	0.9	14.7	16.0	14.2	13.9	15.7	18.1	98.6
KO	Coca-Cola	37.0	20.8	8.1	0.9	17.2	19.1	18.2	18.6	14.9	12.7	19.3
G	Gillette	45.0	9.9	4.9	1.0	17.8	21.1	14.5	15.2	14.2	9.2	22.3
Average		30.4	8.4	3.6	1.4	13.7	15.9	13.2	13.1	12.7	12.1	74.0
Fairly Priced												
ABS	Albertson's	18.3	3.9	0.6	1.8	12.3	10.2	16.8	16.2	16.8	18.1	-23.1
DOV	Dover	19.7	4.9	1.7	1.1	11.2	12.1	27.3	13.8	10.7	14.0	-6.9
MCD	McDonald's	20.4	3.8	2.9	0.7	13.5	13.1	13.9	12.3	14.0	19.2	-14.2
NB	NationsBank	14.7	2.2	2.2	2.1	11.5	8.1	46.2	15.1	10.4	10.7	-30.6
NUE	Nucor	15.4	2.7	1.1	0.8	15.4	10.0	36.7	22.8	11.8	18.0	0.0
MO	Philip Morris	15.5	7.0	1.8	3.8	15.7	6.7	11.5	13.9	18.2	18.2	0.0
SHW	Sherwin-Williams	20.0	3.4	1.1	1.4	11.4	12.0	13.0	11.1	17.4	11.0	-7.2
HWP	Hewlett-Packard	24.7	4.7	1.8	0.8	16.8	15.1	29.7	16.2	13.4	17.2	2.1
Average		18.6	4.1	1.7	1.6	13.5	10.9	24.4	15.2	14.1	15.8	-10.0

Question and Answer Session

Thomas A. Martin, Jr., CFA

Question: How does the DDM work if a company pays no dividend?

Martin: For a company with no cash dividends, such as Microsoft, we have to assume that during the first-stage period of supernormal growth, the company will reinvest all of its earnings back into the company at a high ROE. Then in the second-stage normalization process, or maturity process, we must make assumptions about the point at which the company will be mature enough that it decides to start paying out some dividends, what that rate will be, and how fast the rate of payout will increase to reach some normal payout level. Again, the model makes us explicitly think about where such a company is in its life cycle and what is likely to happen to its products and its profitability over time.

Question: What is the role of beta in these traditional models?

Martin: Beta has no role in the traditional valuation models, with the notable exception of the DDM because the DDM requires the explicit estimation of a discount rate. A discount rate can be derived in a number of ways, one of which is a CAPM approach. If we are going to use CAPM, we also have to use a company beta for each stock being considered.

Beta also can be calculated in several ways. Beta is supposed to be the amount of volatility in the stock price over some period of time relative to some benchmark, but historical betas that are calculated based on price typically are not good predictors of future betas. We all want to know what the relationship will be going forward. So,

many analysts have started using fundamental betas, which are similar to multifactor models based on a company's characteristics, such as debt to equity, sales growth, and margins. Therefore, if we are going to use a CAPM approach, using a fundamental beta to calculate the discount rate probably makes sense.

Question: Do you use normalized earnings in your models?

Martin: A normalized earnings number is a good starting point in using a DDM approach. How we get at that normalized number probably is the key, and it would differ for cyclical companies, for stable companies, and for companies that are currently in distress. One good approach is to have the analysts who follow these companies analyze the fundamentals and try to come up with a normalized number. Another approach is to look at what the company has actually done over some period of time, such as a full business, economic, or profitability cycle, and see if there is some sort of reasonable basis for making our own judgment. Large, stable companies may lend themselves to using past results as a good indicator of the future results because this approach is less subject to analyst forecasting error, but the younger the company or the more fluid the situation, the more our judgment will have to come to bear.

Question: What range of discount rates do you use and how do you apply them to different companies?

Martin: Most users of the DDM solve for the internal rate of return

of the company instead of putting a discount rate into the model and solving for a dollar intrinsic value. The need to estimate the discount rate, which can be a source of potentially large errors, is thereby eliminated.

Question: What is your opinion of price to cash flow and enterprise value to EBITDA (earnings before interest, taxes, depreciation, and amortization) as valuation measures?

Martin: I do not have any real biases for or against any of the valuation models. I think that using a number such as EBITDA is probably better than using a net earnings number, because what we really want to get at is the ongoing capability of a company to generate operating earnings. So, we want to take out as many "nonrecurring" and "management/accounting discretion" items as possible. But even EBITDA is not immune to manipulation. The trouble is that these companies, especially in the S&P 500, change their businesses on an ongoing basis. I saw one study where a substantial portion of the S&P 500's book value had been written off over the past 10 years, and that was one contributor to why ROEs are so much higher and profitability is so much better than in the past. Essentially, managements made a lot of mistakes, and instead of depreciating or amortizing them, they simply wrote them off all at once and hoped that the Street would forget about them. By writing off these expenses, managements figured that they had a better chance of making their earnings estimates and showing good growth rates going forward.

Cash Flow Analysis and Equity Valuation

James A. Ohlson
George O. May Professor of Accounting
Columbia University, Graduate School of Business

Cash flow analysis is not *the* right approach to all valuation exercises, but a focus on cash flow does sharpen many aspects of equity valuation. Using cash flow avoids measurement problems encountered in using an earnings-based valuation approach, and the process of valuing a stock can readily be structured around the concept of free cash flow.

Cash flow analysis may be generally viewed as an extension of the dividend discount model framework with cash flow measures substituted for dividend measures. In truth, cash flow analysis has probably been oversold and is not *the one* right approach to all valuation exercises. The focus on cash flow analysis, however, does sharpen many aspects of equity valuation, and investors and analysts should have a basic understanding of the insights provided by an emphasis on cash flows.

This presentation sets forth a general approach to free cash flow (FCF) analysis, including the justification for using cash flow analysis and some of the practical issues and limitations concerning its application. The presentation also discusses the problems involved in using an earnings-based valuation approach and provides an explanation and example of how to use FCF analysis for stock valuation.

FCF Approach

The basic idea behind any valuation approach is to estimate the intrinsic value of a company. The first step is to split the company into operating and financial activities. So, the value of the company's equity is the present value (PV) of expected FCFs minus the financial obligations, including any passive financial assets. Passive financial assets are those assets that are unnecessary to operate the business, which makes them conceptually similar to financial obligations:

Value = PV of expected FCFs – Net financial obligations,

where

Value	= intrinsic value of equity
FCFs	= cash generated by the business, net of capital expenditures
Net financial obligations	= financial obligations (debt) minus financial assets

In this approach, the PV is determined by a discount factor set equal to the company's weighted-average cost of capital (WACC), which in turn, is a function of the company's cost of equity and after-tax borrowing cost. The cost of equity is typically inferred from the capital asset pricing model or arbitrage pricing theory, which estimate beta, the risk premium, and the risk-free rate. Also, the PV of FCFs usually has two components: the PV of annual FCFs for some specified time horizon, say 7 years or 10 years, plus the PV of the company's "continuing" or "terminal" value as of the end of the time horizon.

Practical issues of implementation arise with this approach; establishing the length of the horizon, for instance, necessarily means that growth issues must be addressed, and estimating continuing value is difficult. Nevertheless, the overall perspective is fairly straightforward: The financial policy is fundamentally irrelevant. The focus is on the business and its ability to generate cash. Debts should be deducted from and financial assets should be added to the estimated intrinsic value of the business. The intrinsic value of the business equates the PV of FCFs so that offsetting the debts and assets yields the value of the equity. Dividend policy, stock buybacks, change in leverage—these elements simply change the risk factor, not cash generation. FCF is the bottom-line cash generated by the business. That cash is then distributed to the creditors and the equityholders in some fashion that depends on the company's financial policy.

Justification for the FCF Approach. Under the assumption that financial policy is irrelevant, the FCF approach is entirely consistent with the dividend discount model, with the economic value added framework, and in fact, with nearly any other valuation approach. FCF has the advantage of being easy to conceptualize, and it allows the investor to focus on what is ultimately important about a company's performance.

Some researchers contend that no alternative to this approach exists; however, alternatives do exist that are conceptually the same, although they may differ at the implementation stage. Researchers also like to point out that by focusing on FCF, accounting problems, especially arbitrary measurements and even manipulations, can be avoided.

The overarching justification for FCF analysis is the notion "cash is king." The problem is that when most people think about that phrase, they think it means that, ultimately, cash is the only component that counts. The correct perspective is that cash is the only component researchers can get a handle on that does not have the potential for measurement error. Although other property rights are equally important, they are much more difficult to value. Therefore, the cash-is-king belief for FCF analysis implies that by focusing on cash, measurement error should not be a factor, in the sense that the numbers should not be sensitive to accounting issues; thus, cash is the only company attribute of long-term relevance.

Practical Questions. The FCF approach, despite its obvious advantages, does engender a number of questions. Practical investment work must *always* deal with the following specific issues:

- How is FCF defined?
- How is WACC measured?
- How is the horizon determined?
- How is continuing value estimated?

Implicit in these questions are three key issues. First, forecasting FCFs is a tricky business. Running the numbers and generating current FCFs are easy tasks, but adding value is difficult when one engages in forecasting FCFs, which is what concerns people: "I am asked to forecast, but I do not have a comparative advantage, so why am I doing it? Can my forecasts be meaningful in any analytical sense?" If analysts have a good understanding of a business and its management strategy, then forecasting might be a good idea. But the problem is, if analysts simply have the company's financial reports and some understanding from various research reports, they may not be able to add much value by forecasting.

The second issue is that, in general, most of the company's value resides in the continuing value, which can make FCF analysis a somewhat disappointing approach. Attempts to estimate continuing value, in turn, usually take one of two forms. One approach is to look at the projected FCFs at the horizon date and then extrapolate the FCF trend using the anticipated growth rate. The second approach, probably used by most analysts, is to assign multiples to the projected net operating profit after taxes (NOPAT) at the horizon year. Typically, the value estimates generated by these two approaches are not that different, but both approaches clearly add uncertainty on top of uncertainty to the analysis—growth in the former case, the multiples in the latter. So, an analyst can engage in detailed forecasting for the next five years and then calculate the PV of FCFs only to find that the PV is dominated by continuing value, which is itself subject to additional uncertainty. All these elaborate forecasts for the next few years might not do much good because their impact on the estimated value is marginal. In other words, the detailed forecasts for the next year or two have virtually no material impact on the bottom line in terms of the estimated intrinsic value.

The third and final issue concerning FCF analysis is that the valuation conclusions are sensitive to the choice of a discount factor. In fact, an analyst's buy or sell conclusion depends substantially on his or her choice of a discount factor as compared with the market's discount factor. In today's market, for example, if an analyst tries to value IBM Corporation using a discount factor in excess of 10 percent, it goes almost without saying that the recommendation will be "sell." The analyst's perception of IBM's economic performance may be optimistic or pessimistic, but this perception is unlikely to be relevant given a discount factor of 10 percent or more.

Implementation Problems. Frankly, and perhaps surprisingly, most people's overall experience in actually using the FCF approach is disappointing. Typically, two reasonable analysts—equally educated, both with a good understanding of the business—can apply the approach and end up with radically different conclusions. They can make FCF forecasts, estimate WACC, specify a horizon, develop continuing values, generate a value, and perform sensitivity analyses. But how was the conclusion reached? Why is the market's conclusion different from that of the FCF analysis? The biggest problem is that once a conclusion is made based on FCF analysis—the stock is cheap or the stock is expensive—analysts have a difficult time trying to disentangle how they arrived at their conclusions compared with the market. Is it because they are more optimistic or less optimistic? Is it because of their discount factor? Is it because of their choice of horizon? Is it their assumption about the continuing value? What about the definition of FCF? In other words, nailing down where the conclusion came from is very difficult.

As a result of these problems, after analysts try the FCF approach for a couple of years, they typically switch to a focus on forecasting earnings. The basic approach is to try to buy earnings cheaply. This approach is straightforward in terms of its various applications. The advantage is that by focusing on earnings, investors can tell what they are doing differently from the rest of the market. Checking anticipated earnings against the market's anticipated earnings is easy, whereas comparing anticipated FCFs with the market's anticipated FCFs is hard indeed.

Problems with Earnings Focus

Have analysts or investors solved their problems by moving from FCFs to earnings? Certainly not. In general, earnings realizations depend substantially on generally accepted accounting principles (GAAP), and companies have discretion and can manage their earnings by using their choice of accounting principles. Perhaps more importantly, they can also manage transactions within the context of GAAP. Investors might suspect, then, that accounting numbers generally, and earnings numbers specifically, are not really indicative of the company's performance. Ultimately, investors are left with the quality of earnings issue, which commingles two tricky factors: (1) the company's real economic activities and the creation of value and (2) the company's application of accounting principles and management of transactions.

The general idea is to determine whether the current earnings are a good indicator of earnings in the future. The company does not even have to be acting mischievously to cause distortions; circumstances may simply create a high quality of earnings or a low quality of earnings. Even under fairly ideal circumstances, determining whether current earnings are, in fact, closely aligned with future earnings is difficult. To the extent that EPS mirrors economic reality, this similarity is often more by chance than by construction. Some telling examples of the difficulties of earnings assessment can be seen in a variety of accounting principle applications that materially affect a company's EPS.

■ *Depreciation and amortization.* The problems with depreciation and amortization are fairly well known. Depreciation schedules are fundamentally arbitrary. The establishment of expected useful lives is enormously flexible, which means that when rapidly growing companies use conservative accounting, they may have heavy depreciation expenses early in the assets' lives. Other companies may find the opposite is true. The result may be a different kind of depreciation expense relative to the standard def-

inition of economic depreciation. For example, if an analyst picked companies at random and looked at their capital expenditures compared with their depreciation expenditures, in several cases, a company's depreciation expenses might well be 30 percent or more of its capital expenditures, even though the company is not growing particularly rapidly. Thus, that company's current capital expenditures would show up as future depreciation expenses 5 or 10 years down the line. The point is that depreciation expenses may not reflect in any way the capital expenditures necessary to maintain a company's productivity or capacity or size. Depreciation expenses are a matter of accounting convention, and because companies can determine useful lives according to their own conventions, an enormous amount of discretion exists with depreciation and amortization expenses.

■ *Restructuring charges.* Restructuring charges are the current accounting curse. Companies like to show earnings growth, and they can do so by simply taking huge write-offs and converting nonrecurring expenses into future recurring profits. If this move does not work to improve earnings, the company can simply do it a second time, as Kimberly-Clark Corporation did recently. Readers of financial statements often think that they do not need to worry about nonrecurring restructuring charges on an income statement because they are nonrecurring. In fact, when incurring huge restructuring charges, companies will show a significant improvement in the profit margin.

■ *Gains and losses.* Gains and losses are essentially the management of transactions and, as such, are very arbitrary. Gains and losses in themselves are nonrecurring, but they do have an impact on the *future* recurring profit margins. Gains and losses can be either phased in or accelerated, depending on how the company structures its transactions. A company that structures a deal properly can accelerate the gain or loss relative to that transaction.

■ *Research and development (R&D) expenditures.* R&D expenditures are becoming more and more important in the U.S. economy. These items are expensed, so growing companies that have R&D expenditures will have consistently understated earnings and apparently high market-to-book ratios.

■ *Postemployment expenses.* Postemployment expenses present specific accounting problems. The postemployment expenses (pensions and postretirement benefits) are quite arbitrary. If a company wants to decrease or increase expenses by 50 percent, in general, that change can be readily accomplished. Fortunately, these items can be found in the footnotes of the financial statements.

This litany of potential earnings distortions, by no means exhaustive, serves to show that earnings do not provide a trouble-free alternative to FCF analysis. Accounting earnings are, in fact, sensitive not only to the application of accounting principles but also to what may be called the management of transactions.

So, how can analysts and investors move past these problems to assess the quality of a company's earnings? The number and variety of suggested approaches to quality-of-earnings analysis is probably limitless, but certain fundamental issues should be kept in mind. Analytical techniques can be used to generate quality-of-earnings ratios, one of the most useful categories being turnover ratios. If a company wants to overstate earnings, then it does so by increasing the profit margin, but the penalty imposed, so to speak, will show up in the turnover ratios, which can be validated analytically or empirically. If a company shows a decrease in asset-turnover ratios, in general, that decrease is an indicator that subsequent profit margins will be lower than current margins.

The footnotes of the financial statements can also help get at quality-of-earnings issues, particularly as those notes detail subtleties in the implementation of accounting principles.

Finally, many, if not most, quality-of-earnings analyses circle back to FCF analysis; out of frustration, analysts and investors decide to focus on cash flows, after having determined that only cash flows are reasonably hard numbers, reasonably free of distortion, and reasonably suitable as a starting point in valuation analysis.

FCF Analysis for Stock Valuation

So, having come full circle from FCF analysis and its difficulties through earnings analysis and its distortions, the idea is that FCF analysis can be used to get at a company's value and thus its stock value. This approach should not be used to replace traditional equity valuation techniques but, rather, as a supplement: a good starting point for trying to understand a company's current market value and possibly whether its stock is overvalued or undervalued. A simple but fairly comprehensive FCF analysis can be conducted in five discrete steps.

Estimate Current FCF. The first step is to estimate the current FCF. Many analysts think that if they want to estimate a company's FCF, they need to look at the cash flow statements; however, the cash flow statements are not needed. The best answer to the problem of how to estimate the current FCF is to define FCF as NOPAT minus the change in the book value of invested capital:

FCF = NOPAT − Δ Invested capital.

NOPAT uses a bottom-up, rather than top-down, approach that starts with net income. Then, any adjustments for foreign currency translation need to be made to get comprehensive income. Next, any interest incurred on debt, net of interest earned on cash and marketable securities, is added; as a practical matter, this net interest can be imputed on the basis of an estimated average after-tax cost. Trying to find the net interest after taxes in the line items is rarely worth the effort, and using a figure such as 4 percent after taxes introduces error that is absolutely minimal.

Invested capital is the book value of equity plus preferred stock plus current and long-term debt minus cash and marketable securities. This calculation can be extended to include accounts receivable and accounts payable to get even more-comprehensive results. If the change in invested capital were not included in the definition, FCF would be simply operating earnings after taxes.

The important insight in this step is that when the current FCF calculation is completed, the resulting number is *not* sensitive to accounting principles. The company may use FIFO or LIFO inventory valuation, straight-line or accelerated depreciation, or other accounting approaches. The choice fundamentally has no impact on the derivation of the current FCF. On the other hand, the FCF result depends heavily on both the company's intrinsic profitability and its intrinsic economic growth.

Estimate Anticipated Growth in FCF. The second step is to estimate the anticipated growth in FCFs. The focus must be on sales and the growth in sales; determining the changes in profit and profit margin is too difficult an accounting calculation, one that relies on complicated aspects of a company's business. Focusing on sales is based on the idea that a company's long-term FCFs are anchored in long-term sales trends that extend from current and recent sales experience. Furthermore, the growth in invested capital should not be materially different from the current growth in sales. If it does, then some adjustments may be appropriate, because growth in invested capital often serves as a leading indicator of future growth in sales. A reasonable, albeit subjective, measure of anticipated growth in FCF puts a one-third weight on recent growth in invested capital and a two-thirds weight on recent growth in sales.

Infer Expected Return on the "Unlevered Firm." After estimating the current FCFs and the anticipated growth in FCFs, the present value of the FCFs can be calculated as

$$PV \text{ of FCF} = \frac{1 + \text{Growth}}{r - \text{Growth}} (\text{Current FCF}),$$

where r is the expected return or discount factor. This equation is essentially the constant-growth dividend discount model with FCF substituted for dividends.

The discount factor cannot be assumed but, rather, needs to be inferred: What is the anticipated return given the current FCFs and the anticipated growth rate? The proper procedure is to look at current FCFs, visualize future growth, and try to infer the implied return on that kind of investment as follows. The value of the firm is equal to the market capitalization of equity plus net debt, which in turn, should be equal to the PV of the FCFs:

$$\text{Value of the firm} = \text{Market capitalization of equity}$$
$$+ \text{Net debt}$$
$$= \text{PV of FCFs.}$$

Realizing that the value of the firm equals the PV of FCFs allows the anticipated discount factor, r, to be inferred:

$$\text{Value of the firm} = \frac{1 + \text{Growth}}{r - \text{Growth}} (\text{Current FCF}),$$

and

$$r = \text{Growth} + (1 + \text{Growth}) \frac{\text{Current FCF}}{\text{Value of the firm}}$$
$$= \text{Growth} + \frac{\text{Current FCF}}{\text{Value of the firm}}$$
$$+ \text{Growth} \left(\frac{\text{Current FCF}}{\text{Value of the firm}} \right).$$

Thus, the anticipated return is a function of the anticipated growth, the current FCF, and the value of the firm (unlevered). In this calculation, however, the value of

$$\text{Growth} \left(\frac{\text{Current FCF}}{\text{Value of the firm}} \right)$$

is virtually always immaterial, so the anticipated return is equal to the anticipated sales growth plus the cash yield of the company, or

$$r = \text{Growth} + \frac{\text{Current FCF}}{\text{Value of the firm}}.$$

Therefore, by picking a growth rate and looking at the current FCFs relative to capitalization, the expected future return, r, can be determined, given that the current market price is considered valid. It follows that r can be used as part of a buy/sell decision: A relatively high r suggests a buy signal, and a relatively low r suggests a sell signal.

Calculate Levered r. The fourth step is a further refinement of the general procedure: calculating the r value for the levered rather than the unlevered firm. The expected return on equity relates to the previously derived r, but adjustments are required to reflect the existence of leverage.

$$\text{Equity-}r = r + \text{Leverage} \times [r - BC(AT)],$$

where

Equity-r	=	expected return after adjustment for leverage (i.e., expected equity return)
r	=	expected return on (unlevered) firm
Leverage	=	Net debt/Market value of equity
BC(AT)	=	after-tax interest (or borrowing) cost (4 percent)

These calculations are routine. If a company has leverage, then the implied return on an equity investment will be higher, depending on the borrowing cost and the extent of the leverage.

Relate Equity-r to Risk. The fifth step is a final refinement to make some kind of implicit risk adjustment. One approach is to run regression models that use beta to explain the inferred equity value. The residuals can then be examined as indications that a stock is overvalued or undervalued. As an alternative procedure, an analyst may simply compare Equity-r with some direct assessment of the appropriate benchmark for a company's equity risk. For example, if an analyst is comfortable that a reasonable risk-adjusted discount factor should not exceed 8 percent for a company and the implied Equity-r equals 10 percent, then the analyst should also be comfortable with a buy decision. Regardless of approach, the message is that somewhere in the overall process, a risk adjustment needs to be made, and adjusting for risk is probably the last step, given that it is very difficult and exceedingly subjective.

Whatever the risk adjustment method used, the point of risk adjustment is clear. Given that the implied Equity-r equals X percent, does X percent look attractive relative to the analyst's perception of the underlying risk and relative to other opportunities available? If two firms are deemed equally risky, then the one with the larger Equity-r makes the better investment. Furthermore, if two firms have approximately the same Equity-r, then the one judged to be less risky makes the best investment.

FCF Example

An example can help illustrate the simple yet comprehensive nature of FCF analysis. **Table 1** is from Colgate-Palmolive Company's December 31, 1996, annual report. The focus here is entirely on Steps 1, 2, and 3, which are reasonably objective in nature and thus generalizable. Steps 4 and 5 would require more subjective judgments on the part of the individual analyst performing the analysis. (For this particular company, it also turns out that Step 4 is unnecessary because the leverage is immaterial.)

Table 1. Colgate-Palmolive Financial Statement Data, December 31, 1996
($ millions except as noted)

Item	1996	1995	1994	1993	1992
Sales	8,749.00	8,358.20	7,587.90	7,141.30	7,007.20
Percent annual growth	5%	10%	6%		
Growth in 5 years	25%				
Annual average (geometric)	6%				
Growth in recent 3 years	15%				
Annual average (geometric)	7%				
Common stock equivalents	1,641.40	1,276.30	1,414.50		
Preferred stock	392.70	403.50	408.40		
Long-term debt	2,786.80	2,992.00	1,751.50		
Short-term debt	282.70	241.40	207.90		
Deduct: Cash	248.20	208.80	169.90		
Deduct: Marketable securities	59.60	47.80	47.60		
Invested capital	4,795.80	4,656.60	3,564.80		
Percent annual growth	3%	31%			
Growth in recent 3 years	35%				
Annual average (geometric)	16%				
Net income	635.00	172.00			
Preferred dividends	21.40	21.60			
Net income to common stock (NICS)	613.60	150.40			
Adjustment for comprehensive earnings	(21.70)	(73.70)			
Comprehensive NICS	591.90	76.70			
Net interest expense (after tax)[a]	110.47	119.07			
NOPAT	723.77	217.37			
Change in net invested capital	139.20	1,091.80			
Free cash flow	584.57	(874.43)			
Percent annual growth	(167)%				
12/96 closing price ($)	46.125				
Number of shares	294.27				
Market capitalization	13,573.20				
RNOA	16%	7%			
RNOA(CO)	15%	5%			
ROCE	42%	11%			
ROCE(CO)	41%	6%			

[a]4 percent (debt minus cash and marketable securities).

Source: Based on data from Colgate-Palmolive Company 1996 annual report.

■ *Step 1.* NOPAT for 1996 is calculated as $723.77 million, starting with net income and adjusting for foreign currency earnings and financial items. The invested capital is the sum of the book values of equity, preferred stock, long-term debt, and short-term debt less cash and marketable securities. The change in invested capital from 1995 to 1996 was $139.20 million. 1996 FCF was, therefore, $584.57 million ($723.77 million – $139.20 million).

■ *Step 2.* In 1996, sales were $8,749.00 million; the five-year average growth trend in sales has been 6 percent; and the three-year trend has been 7 percent. A reasonable range for growth in sales, therefore, is 5 to 8 percent. This range also corresponds, at least roughly, to the growth in invested capital.

■ *Step 3.* The market capitalization of equity at the end of 1996 was $13,573.20 million. Net debt was $3,154.40 million ($4,795.80 million – $1.641.40 million). Colgate-Palmolive's value, then, was $16,727.60 million ($13,573.20 million + $3,154.40 million). The 1996 FCF was $584.57 million, so the company's cash yield was 3.5 percent ($584.57 million/$16,727.60 million). With an expected growth rate of, say, 7 percent (from Step 1), then, the unlevered return *r* becomes 10.5 percent (7 percent growth + 3.5 percent cash yield).

This analysis makes clear that an investor's expected return has two components: growth and cash yield. What a company does not generate in growth it must generate in current FCF. What it does not provide in current FCF it must provide in growth.

Conclusion

FCF analysis provides a useful and relatively simple starting point for equity valuation. The approach has several limitations, however, including one shared by all valuation techniques: Estimating growth, which is at the heart of the matter, cannot be avoided and can never be other than subjective. The analyst or investor who can systematically estimate growth with precision has a powerful advantage indeed. But for the vast majority who do not have that advantage, FCF analysis can still organize a thought process that links the company's performance with that of its stock. FCF analysis can be refined in many ways, but in its purest form, it has a virtue not shared by all valuation approaches: FCF provides the simplest possible picture of the potential benefits from investing in a company.

Question and Answer Session

James A. Ohlson

Question: Why do you exclude changes in working capital from your calculation?

Ohlson: It is *not* excluded! Remember that I am working backward, so to speak, from the entire balance sheet. Remember also that debits equal credits; thus, the change in invested capital from a financial perspective must, by construction, equal the change in invested capital from an operating perspective. One can use either approach, of course. The number will always be the same as long as we are comprehensive and mutually exclusive in the treatment of the line items in the balance sheet.

Question: How can the FCF approach be applied to a rapidly growing small company that is generating negative cash or to a company that is acquisition driven?

Ohlson: It cannot be applied very well in the case of rapid growth and negative cash. Whenever we try to value a company that has a growth factor in excess of the discount factor, we will have very difficult problems, because no growth rate can exceed the discount factor forever. Somewhere along the line, we have to make a call as to when that growth rate is going to

level off, decline, and ultimately go below the discount factor. Even this approach to the growth problem does not completely solve the problem of how to value a currently negative cash generator. This kind of case always poses daunting valuation problems.

An acquisition-driven company poses similar problems: If I believe that acquisitions are going to change a company's intrinsic economic profitability, then I am saying that the current financial statements are not going to help me anticipate and understand the future financial statements. To the extent that the current statements cannot give me a sense of the future statements, I have no or little basis for the FCF approach. That limitation, I would argue, applies to any valuation approach.

Question: How do you justify using these methods, which are long-term oriented, when Wall Street is so short-term oriented?

Ohlson: The way I think about all of these valuation techniques is that they are neither engineering approaches nor *the* right or best approach. They are just different schemes to organize our thinking. I think it is dangerous to look for the Holy Grail of valuation. That

level of certainty is not there, and it is never going to be there. Some of the key parameters that we have to put into any of these models are too close to figments of the imagination to take the models that seriously.

Question: Is cash flow truly independent of the accounting method used?

Ohlson: Yes. If you calculate FCF the way I outlined, it does not depend on the depreciation expense. Why? Because, on the one hand, depreciation expense has an impact on NOPAT and, on the other hand, depreciation expense has an impact on the change in invested capital. The two impacts are precisely offsetting, as are the effects of other accruals, such as pension expense. There are exceptions, of course, such as executive compensation options, but in general, accounting problems do not arise when we calculate FCF. The exceptions refer to transactions in which capital contributions and deductions are improperly measured. Options are one example, and the accounting for employee stock ownership plans is another. It is rarely worth the effort to try to straighten out these items, although it can generally be done.

Using EVA in Equity Analysis

Alfred G. Jackson, CFA
Director of Global Research
Credit Suisse First Boston

Few analytical methods can contribute more than economic value added (EVA) to the task of picking stocks that outperform the market. EVA addresses a wide variety of key valuation questions for a company, ranging from whether capital is used efficiently to which business segments create value.

The mission of investment professionals is to pick stocks that outperform the market. Few, if any, methods pick stocks as well as economic value added (EVA) analysis, in which EVA is defined as the difference between a company's net operating profit after taxes (NOPAT) and it's cost of invested capital. Simply estimating and studying EVA can enhance analysis in many ways. This presentation discusses using EVA to determine whether the incremental return on invested capital (ROIC) exceeds the weighted-average cost of capital (WACC), whether capital is used efficiently in the company, whether high-return businesses subsidize low-return businesses, which geographical regions of a company's operations add value to that company, which business segments exceed a company's WACC and create value, and finally, which stocks are likely to outperform the market.

Return on Invested Capital

From an operating perspective, invested capital is the sum of net assets (net working capital plus net property, plant, and equipment plus goodwill plus other assets) a company uses; from a financing perspective, invested capital is the sum of capital invested (total debt plus deferred taxes plus other liabilities plus preferred stock plus common equity) to fund assets. Other modifications to invested capital are certainly possible; for example, at Credit Suisse First Boston, we make about 15 different adjustments to invested capital for certain companies in certain industries to reflect such items as capitalized research and development costs and accumulated goodwill amortization. We also add back write-offs; that capital may have disappeared for generally accepted accounting principles or for purposes of calculating EPS, but it is still in invested capital.

The incremental return on invested capital is a function of the return generated, defined as NOPAT (Sales − Operating expenses − Taxes) for a given period relative to the difference between the invested capital used at the beginning of that period and the period-ending invested capital. One word of caution is in order: ROIC frequently displays big swings from year to year; a three-, four-, or even five-year average gives a more accurate sense of real trends in a company's incremental ROIC than a one- or two-year average.

ROIC is a leading indicator of stock price performance, especially in turnaround situations, and the recent stock price performance of Wal-Mart Stores is a good case in point. During the 1990–96 period, Wal-Mart's EPS continued to grow strongly, but its ROIC—the capital that is used in the business on the margin—declined dramatically, from 25 percent in 1990 to 6 percent in 1996. Analysts should have looked at ROIC, not EPS, when the stock price reached a new high in 1993, and they should have asked what was wrong with Wal-Mart, not what was right. Although Wal-Mart stock appreciated more than 6,000 percent from 1981 to 1993, by the early 1990s, Wal-Mart was clearly not using capital effectively on the margin, and as early as 1991, EVA would have shown that Wal-Mart stock would underperform the market for the next several years. If analysts had used an EVA analysis of Wal-Mart in 1990, they would have seen that the stock price implied that the company's ROIC would exceed its WACC by 700 basis points (bps) for the next 17 years. Half of the value in that stock price was to come from things that the company had not yet done. Clearly, these were untenable implications, and in fact, during the 1991–96 period, Wal-Mart's stock price depreciated at a compound rate of about 3 percent, at a time when the market was appreciating dramatically.

The reverse is true at Procter & Gamble, where ROIC increased from 1.5 percent in 1991 to 24 percent in 1996, with especially dramatic increases in 1992 and 1993. Procter & Gamble's stock price had a compound growth rate of about 22 percent during the 1991–96 period. EPS, however, did not rise accordingly, and EPS growth only began to catch up with the returns in capital later in that five-year period. The lesson is that ROIC, not EPS, is a leading indicator for whether a stock will perform well. For both Wal-Mart and Procter & Gamble, EPS gave a misleading signal. EPS growth was strong at Wal-Mart and masked a deteriorating ROIC situation; EPS growth was weak at Procter & Gamble and hid an improving ROIC situation.

Capital Efficiency

Comparing a company's ROIC with its WACC for a given period provides insight into that company's capital efficiency. A company's WACC is the weighted cost of its invested capital; the cost of debt is a function of market yields, and the cost of equity can be determined in a capital asset pricing model framework. During the 1989–94 period, CPC International and Kellogg Company each invested nearly $1 billion in capital expenditures, but they achieved markedly different results. CPC's stock price in that five-year period went up 42 percent, and Kellogg's stock price went up 79 percent. The telling contrast was the growth in Kellogg's NOPAT compared with that of CPC. In that five-year period, Kellogg's NOPAT increased $150 million; CPC's NOPAT increased about one-third of that amount—$55 million. Why? Kellogg's ROIC far exceeded its WACC, by almost 400 bps, whereas CPC was actually using capital at a negative return. How efficiently a company uses its capital determines how well its stock performs; because of the dramatically different levels of capital efficiency, no one should be surprised that CPC's stock went up only 42 percent while Kellogg's rose 79 percent.

Gateway 2000 and Dell Computer Corporation both sell made-to-order personal computers (PCs) to consumers and businesses. At the beginning of the 1995–97 period, Gateway and Dell were essentially identical companies, at least on a financial basis. Capital turnover (annual sales divided by average stockholder equity) at both was about 9 times, and working capital turnover, which reflects the amount of working capital needed to maintain a given level of sales, was 10 times at Dell and 15 times at Gateway. Gateway's turnover ratios were unchanged by 1997, although Dell's capital turnover increased to 31 times

and working capital turnover increased to 85 times, which led to a dramatic increase in operating margins. Both companies were in a business that the market favored, but Dell's stock price appreciated 12.5 times during the period and Gateway's stock price appreciated only 3.5 times. Again, how efficiently capital is used, in this case Dell's remarkable turnover of capital, directly affects stock price.

Subsidization

EVA can also show whether the large profits of one division are subsidizing the poor returns of another. In the 1989–94 period, General Mills was essentially in two businesses—food and restaurants. The food business earned 75 percent of the company's total profit and realized a 23 percent return on invested capital; the restaurant business earned only 25 percent of the company's profit and a 7 percent return on capital, but it received nearly 50 percent of General Mills's total capital expenditures. This situation illustrates cross-subsidization gone the wrong way; EVA would have shown early on that the high-return food business was subsidizing the low-return, no-growth restaurant business. Finally, management at General Mills split the company into two parts. The restaurant business, renamed Darden Restaurants, became an independent company; it cut capital expenditures dramatically, reduced spending on experimental concepts, used cash flow much more effectively, and in general, no longer spent money as freely as when it was subsidized by the food business.

Operations by Region

EVA can be used to look at various operations by geographical region. CPC International, with franchise brand names such as Knorr soup and Hellmann's mayonnaise, established a huge presence in European markets, and many analysts thought Europe to be the crown jewel of CPC. In 1993, for instance, Europe represented 30 percent of operating income generated at CPC, and an analyst looking only at CPC's operating income in 1993 would have said, "Europe is a pretty good business—30 percent operating income, great brand names. It is probably a value driver." In fact, Europe was a value destroyer for CPC. European operations realized an economic profit in 1993 of –9 percent; in other words, Europe destroyed 9 percent of the value at this company in 1993. By contrast, CPC's North American business, although it had only 45 percent of the operating profits, accounted for 75 percent of the value creation. So, the North American business created value and the European business destroyed value. Combining operating income with the capital that is used in the business, being sure that each operation is charged for the capital it uses, gives a much different picture of value from what would be seen by simply looking at earnings or the operating income from any division.

Business Segments

EVA is useful for examining a company's various segments. For example, in 1995, 75 percent of Compaq Computer Corporation's sales came from nonserver businesses, but the server business represented 76 percent of Compaq's value creation. The server ROIC was about 63 percent, and the PC ROIC was about 16 percent, both compared with a WACC of 15 percent. Compaq was a server company, not a PC company, and to recommend the stock as a PC stock would have been misleading. Only when Compaq's management began to free up the capital in the distribution system of the PC business, where no value was being created, did the stock begin to look attractive to our analyst. The EVA approach pushed management and investors alike to ask where Compaq's value was really being created and when problems in the PC business would be addressed.

The Compaq analysis also illustrates the difficulty in estimating a divisional cost of capital, in this case for the server business. Obviously, the divisional WACC is not in the annual report or 10-K, but our analyst at Credit Suisse First Boston pieced together information from a variety of sources, arrived at a WACC estimate, and told Compaq's chief financial officer (CFO) that that estimate would be published. Faced with that eventuality, most CFOs will give the analyst a good sense of whether the WACC estimate is reasonable.

Stock Selection

Finally, EVA can be used to help select stocks; such is the case in a value dynamic framework used at Credit Suisse First Boston. That framework, a subset of which is depicted in **Figure 1**, is a database of about 600 companies. We compare a company's value with its ROIC. Essentially, higher ROIC values result in higher market values for the company. Figure 1 simply indicates a strong correlation (R^2 is 74 percent) between ROIC and value; the higher the returns, the higher the value. Because it ties stock price to ROIC, the framework represented in Figure 1 is particularly useful when combined with traditional fundamental analysis. For example, Figure 1 suggests that both value and growth investors can use EVA to pick stocks.

Figure 1. Value versus Return Framework

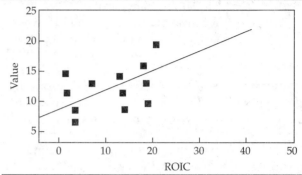

Note: Value is measured as enterprise value divided by incremental capital.

Value investing. The left-hand side of Figure 1 reveals companies with relatively low returns and low valuations; the question is: Will returns, and thus valuations, improve? Unocal serves as a good example. In the context of Figure 1, Unocal had low returns and low value several years ago, but the company planned to reduce its capital expenditures in certain businesses and invest more money in its international gas businesses. Selecting Unocal then was a good move; the company's returns improved, and so did its valuation.

Growth investing. Companies at the far right-hand side of Figure 1, such as Microsoft Corporation, represent high returns and valuations; the questions now are: Can this company continue to have high incremental return? Can this company sustain those returns? Perhaps a company with a return of 20 percent is substantially undervalued; the analyst needs to ask what catalyst would actually force that company back toward the average valuation for that level of return. Conversely, if a stock is substantially overvalued, the analyst needs to ask what could go wrong to make that company revert to the mean.

Conclusion

The analytical uses of EVA run the gamut from returns on incremental capital and capital efficiency to subsidization and segment analysis. For the investment professional, no use is more important than stock selection, and EVA indicates not only the value of a stock today but also what that stock can be worth in the future. Almost every firm on Wall Street uses traditional measures—P/E, EPS growth, and the like—to analyze companies. These measures do not even begin to tell the story in stock valuation; the full story is available only with the use of EVA. Fortunately, EVA is a suitable analytical tool to bring to bear with nearly all industries and the vast majority of companies.

Question and Answer Session

Alfred G. Jackson

Question: What is the time frame of EVA? Has it shortened management's time perspective?

Jackson: Implied in the question may be the notion that, because EVA is measured every year, management has only a one-year expectational horizon. A true EVA system, fully implemented, builds in a long time horizon; even EVA-based compensation is typically paid out over several years, so management cannot hide from its mistakes. There are several good examples of firms that have successfully implemented EVA for the long term. Briggs & Stratton has used EVA for eight years, and stock prices have performed relatively well in that period; Equifax has used EVA for seven years, and changes in the company have been clear as it has gone through the various stages of implementation.

Question: Is the change in direction of EVA more important than the level?

Jackson: Yes. A company going from negative to positive catches the investor's attention more and has a greater effect on the stock price, at least in the short term, than does going from positive to a bit more positive.

Question: How have your clients accepted EVA? Will acceptance and adoption of EVA ever be widespread?

Jackson: Our clients, in general, have accepted it very well, probably because we use EVA not for the numbers that come out of the model but for what the model tells us—an understanding of companies and their business models. A positive or negative EVA is a very interesting data point, but EVA's main contribution is to give analysts and investors a better understanding of the business model. The more we can understand about where a company is going, the better investment decision we can make.

Will it be universally accepted on the sell side? Absolutely not. We now have most of our analysts using this tool to look at the companies that they cover, but my sense is that most sell-side firms have not even begun that process.

Question: What adjustments in culture and organization are necessary for a company adopting EVA?

Jackson: The companies that have had the biggest problems adopting EVA are those that do so in name only. For instance, management says EVA has been implemented, but the compensation system is still based on EPS or some measure of return on assets. Unless the CEO and the board agree to full implementation and actually follow through, little good will come of the effort. Domtar, a Canadian paper company, is a good example. It implemented

EVA in 1995, had terrific results, and banked big EVA bonuses for future payout to employees. In 1996, results were very poor, and management reduced the EVA bank accordingly.

What the employees said to the company was, "Quantitatively, we didn't do that well. But we did those qualitative things you asked us to do, and you're not paying us for it. You're even taking it out of the EVA bank." So, Domtar's management, in its enthusiastic implementation, set up employee expectations in the first year but took a step back from the program in the second year. Companies may well fear that, if they turn their entire compensation system over to EVA, they are captive to a model or a framework they cannot control, but full and persistent implementation is the key.

Question: Does the use of EVA deter capital investment?

Jackson: I hope it deters inefficient capital investment, that it penalizes companies that invest their capital at returns below their WACC. EVA should stop those acquisitions that are destroying value, which some financial studies suggest may include two-thirds of all acquisitions consummated. EVA can add an aspect of rationality to corporate management.

New Methodologies for Equity Analysis and Valuation

Patrick O'Donnell
Chief of Global Equity Research
Putnam Investment Management

Based on sound theory and with clear **advantages** over traditional measures, present value methodologies for equity valuation **offer** investment firms the potential for making better valuation judgments. Widespread **use** of present value methodologies is likely but not assured; they are complex, sometimes **difficult** to implement, and often threatening to entrenched investment cultures.

The single most important change taking place today in equity research may well be the globalization of the scope of research departments. Equity research groups are increasingly responsible for valuing stocks in a wide range of markets—from emerging markets to the more efficient major markets—and for making cross-market comparisons. Globalization is taking place in the traditional growth and value styles of investing but is also spawning new kinds of investment products. These changes pose exciting challenges for analysts, who must find ways to deal with the increased level of complexity they face in valuing stocks around the world.

This presentation discusses two of the new equity valuation methodologies—economic value added (EVA) and discounted cash flow (DCF)—that have particular appeal in global analysis. These two approaches and their growing multitude of brethren might loosely be termed present value (PV) disciplines. This presentation focuses on the reasons that those methodologies are attracting attention, what they have in common, their advantages and disadvantages compared with traditional valuation measures, what potential benefits they offer, what implementation problems they pose, and what the future may hold for their use.

Appeal

Over the past few years, the subject of value has seen increased coverage in books and articles in top-flight academic journals. This increase was spurred by the 1991 publication of G. Bennett Stewart's book *The Quest for Value*. As shown in **Figure 1**, the number of LEXIS–NEXIS citations on EVA alone has increased from 3 in 1990 to nearly 300 as of December 1997.

The new methodologies are being marketed by consulting and accounting firms and have been well received by the global corporate world. Corporate managers during the 1980s became sensitized to the fact that their jobs, stock options, and economic fortunes were jeopardized whenever the public market placed a low price on the assets entrusted to them. Since then, managers have become very receptive to any discipline or methodology that will help them show investors that they have improved the economic returns on the assets that they manage.

The new methodologies lend themselves to assessment of a business manager's success. EVA, in fact, was primarily invented as a tool for managers; the subtitle of Stewart's book is *A Guide for Senior Managers*. EVA makes sense as a tool for company managers, who can apply it consistently across the operating divisions in their firms and who have access to detailed financial statements that permit creation of accurate cash-based financial statements.

Modern theory has outgrown the old approaches. Finance professors have in some instances stopped teaching the valuation yardsticks of the previous generation, such as P/E, price-to-sales (P/S), and return-on-equity approaches. In fact, Putnam Investment Management recruits heavily from one business school where the students are not allowed to discuss P/E but, rather, only the results from PV methodologies. This change is symptomatic of an ongoing evolutionary trend, both in academic circles and among practitioners, toward new methodologies. The

Figure 1. Number of EVA Citations in LEXIS–NEXIS, 1990–97

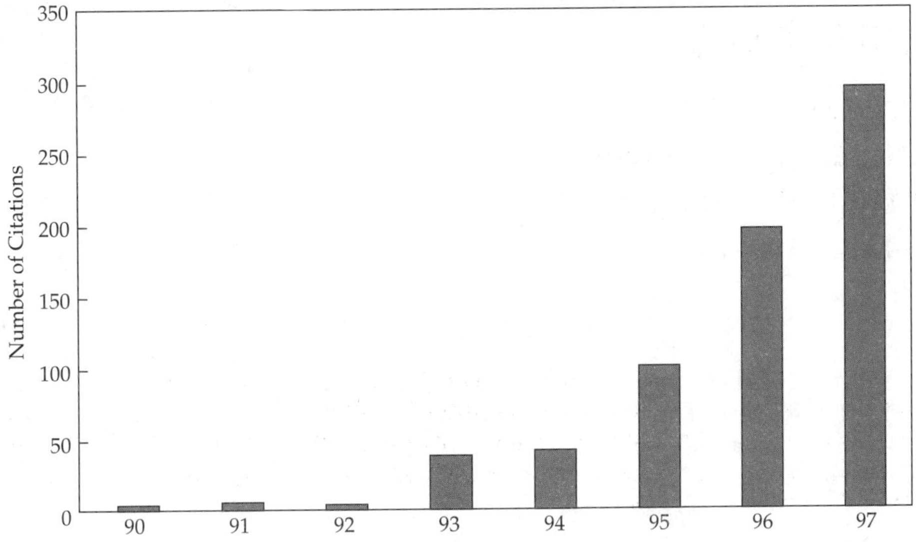

Note: 1997 data are as of December 1997.

old methodologies focus on earnings-based measures, with some consideration of yield; 5 or 10 years ago, the dominant valuation approaches included P/E, P/S, and among a distinct minority of practitioners, the dividend discount model (DDM). The new methodologies focus much more carefully on the creation or destruction of value; they emphasize the future benefits from investing capital now. The PV calculations permit analysts to value the cash flows from a firm as it now exists and from its use of cash and its financing capability, whether that capability is used to expand the business, repurchase stock, or pay dividends.

Such an approach is based on rather abstract assertions: The basic raw material of industrial capitalism is capital, and the basic product of industrial capitalism is enhanced capital; industrial capitalism is itself a transforming engine that takes capital and makes it more valuable. Less abstractly, a successful firm turns raw materials into cars or refrigerators or microchips. The process is driven by labor and creativity. (Indeed, creativity is the principal capital in knowledge-based firms.) Analysts spend much of their time trying to figure out how firms, the engines of capitalism, work and whether the market is putting the right price tag on the firm relative to its real economic value. This "real economic value" is easy for a professor to describe as "the present value of all future cash returns to shareholders," but it is a devilishly tricky number for analysts to calculate, which is where the PV methodologies help.

The PV approaches have several common components: (1) a period of forecasted cash flows, (2) a period of forecasted maturation or reversion to mean

economic returns (expressed as cash flows), and (3) a discounting factor that consists of the risk-free rate plus an equity risk premium plus some adjustment for the riskiness of the firm. The technical applications of various PV approaches vary, but in essence, the discount rate is the functional equivalent of the cost of capital.

The PV approaches provide a transparent framework within which the analyst can work and, equally importantly, can present his or her thinking to colleagues. The forecast period, as we implement the process at Putnam, is five years, for which the analyst creates a demand model for a company's products, leading to a revenue model and a cost model, which helps forecast operating income. A cash flow model extends from the model of business operations. The critical issue to be addressed in cash flow is the analyst's estimate of management's use of cash available for reinvestment or for payment to shareholders, either in the form of a direct dividend or via stock repurchase.

The new PV approaches borrow heavily from some of their predecessors. The DCF method might be seen as an evolutionary successor to the old-style DDM. The concept of present value is, of course, not new, neither is the idea of expecting a business to earn a satisfactory return on capital. The EVA and DCF disciplines do, however, focus analysts' attention explicitly on economic earnings, rather than on accounting earnings, and on the productive use of capital, rather than on the growth of reported income per share. These disciplines are also more systematic and sophisticated than the ratio approaches (i.e., P/E and P/S) but, admittedly, at the cost of being more labor intensive. In addition, the PV approaches force disciplined thinking and conscious evaluation of appropriate discount rates. Significantly, they provide a lens to look through various accounting systems at underlying real economic phenomena.

Finally, with dollars pouring into equity managers and widespread underperformance, the pressure has increased to find a "competitive edge," and the new methodologies offer that promise, at least in theory. They are not a "magic bullet" or the next "genie out of the bottle," but they do offer a framework by which to maintain consistency and discipline in a valuation approach that focuses on enhancing the value of capital. It is, one easily imagines, confidence inspiring for a client to know that an asset manager is bringing his or her creativity to a promising valuation discipline.

Commonalities

These new disciplines, first and foremost, share as a common focus the cost of capital and adjusted return on capital, which is a simpler concept than it is sometimes made to sound. Imagine that a firm is borrowing money from a bank at a specified rate, or "rent." The bank has set the rate to reflect its required return and its assessment of the risk that it will not get its money back. The process is analogous to the equity market's setting of a rate for a firm's cost of equity that reflects investors' consensus expectations for the firm's prospects. The equity market might require a 15 percent return from a technology company whose cash flows it believes are more uncertain than those of a food company, which it charges a notional rent that is more like 10 percent.

Imagine that an analyst's work leads to the insight that, for example, a large technology company has rather predictable cash flows, even though it is generally regarded as having substantial exposure to the business cycle. Using a DCF approach, the analyst might use a lower risk premium for that company than the market seems to be using. If the analyst is right, the rewards, in terms of investment outperformance, can be huge. The PV disciplines can lead to insight that gives the investor a competitive advantage over other investors who are simply using a P/E approach. Both methods ultimately depend on subjective judgments, but the PV approaches make the valuation decision a more multidimensional one.

The PV approaches also all share a rejection of accounting measures based on generally accepted accounting principles (GAAP) or any of the various national accounting standards. They all basically move toward a cash-based view of a business. Several rely on some kind of proprietary, idiosyncratic, or unique approach to adjusting reported financial statements. Many of these methodologies are sold as commercial services and rely on proprietary databases (i.e., historical data that have been reformulated to be consistent with the discipline that is being sold).

The vendor-supplied methodologies, because they use a PV approach to valuing future returns, do not take analysts out of the forecasting business, although they will typically provide a "naive" set of forecasts. Without exception, however, these disciplines rely on forecasting future cash flows and returns, which can be provided by the client analyst.

The PV approaches also rely on a risk adjustment factor, which is where the various approaches may be differentiated to some extent and where the controversies still reside. The risk adjustment factor may be termed the cost of capital or the discount rate. Theory says the three components of the discount rate, or the risk adjustment factor, are (1) the risk-free rate, (2) an equity risk premium, and (3) a company-specific risk premium. Practitioners who have been applying the PV approaches have raised all sorts of interesting analytical questions, none of which challenge the basic validity of the approach but which do have some implications for the way in which a DCF is applied in practice.

Some experienced investors, for example, question whether an equity risk premium actually exists. "Are stocks inherently riskier than bonds," they ask, "simply because they have returned more than bonds for as long as statistics have been kept?" Finance theorists have asserted that the outperformance of stocks means the market has required a higher return from stocks than bonds. Those of a more practical bent argue that the historical record simply illustrates that stocks are a better investment than bonds over time. Whether one uses an equity risk premium actually makes little practical difference, because most participants in the money management business are trying to rank stocks according to relative attractiveness. As long as analysts are consistent in using discount rates, even leaving out an equity risk premium, such relative rankings should be logical.

Another controversy focuses on whether the company-specific risk premium should be set by using the capital asset pricing model and beta. Use of a historical beta implies that risk equals volatility. But is that implication true? Perhaps risk is represented by the statement, "I am sorry, Ms. Smith; I lost your money," but volatility is represented by the statement, "Ms. Smith, I hope you were not planning to pay the rent this month with that money." Perhaps a time value of money exists in equity valuation and risk assessment that is too often ignored. Resolving these questions—how to define risk and whether to use historical or prospective risk measures—is an important part of using the new methodologies; fortunately, the methodologies themselves provide a good framework for the discussions that are so critical to resolving the questions.

Finally, the new methodologies, by their very focus on future benefits, share an explicitly longer-term view of a firm's prospects than do the more traditional measures. Ratio analysis tends to depend heavily on historical norms and can easily miss changes taking place in companies, as well as the valuation implications of those changes. Because the PV approaches require explicit forecasting of important future variables for several years, at a minimum, they almost force the analyst to have a greater reliance on future rather than present results.

Advantages and Disadvantages

Although the new methodologies offer substantial advantages over traditional, multiples-based approaches, they also carry some disadvantages.

Advantages. First, they provide a consistent and clear framework for valuation. Therefore, growth and value analysts, large-capitalization and small-capitalization managers, domestic and global investors—all can talk at the same time about the same critical variables. Second, the new methodologies do not depend on GAAP financial reporting.

Third, the financial inputs are consistent, allowing more-realistic company-to-company, industry-to-industry, and cross-border comparisons. The final advantage, which is potentially the most substantial but also the most difficult to make real, is that these disciplines can make the relationship between expected or forecasted returns and the fair price for the stock quantifiable, specific, and sometimes even transparent. The primary advantage of PV-based disciplines, in fact, is the ability to say that a given asset is intrinsically undervalued, overvalued, or fairly valued.

Disadvantages. These new methodologies require detailed, explicit analyses and forecasts covering several periods, say five years, and thus are labor intensive and expensive. At Putnam, the ongoing additional expense probably amounts to the cost of several full-time-equivalent analysts. Another disadvantage is that for some investment approaches, these disciplines do not provide a lot of help; for instance, these methodologies do not give much insight with respect to momentum or sector rotation, and they can be difficult to apply to very high-growth, small-cap companies. For such companies, which often rely on a single product or limited range of products, the investment and valuation decisions

are binary: If the product fails, the stock is certainly overvalued; if it succeeds, forecasting the degree of success can be very difficult but the stock is more likely to be undervalued. The final disadvantage is that these disciplines do not provide any better final protection against self-deception than the old methods; an analyst's biggest enemy is her or his own illusion of expertise. These disciplines, with their elegant theory and myriad adjustments, can look very official, almost canonical, and the possibility arises of making a substantial cognitive error by ascribing truth where it does not in fact exist.

Benefits for Investment Firms

No investment firm would need any help if it were consistently good at understanding how companies were improving or degrading their use of cash and available financing for projects, stock repurchases, or dividends. In addition, no investment firm would need help if it could consistently understand when companies were improving or degrading their returns from existing assets, either by improving those assets or by making capital-allocation decisions—starving assets of capital or selling them off.

But most, if not all, investment firms have their ups and downs in these processes, and using the new methodologies offers potential real benefits. For instance, they can help in diagnostic screening. One of the biggest challenges in the investment business is improving the "signal-to-noise ratio," and the first step for a firm is deciding which stocks analysts should investigate out of the universe of more than 40,000 traded stocks in the world. Eliminating all the stocks that do not trade well and the ones that are semi-private reduces the set to about 5,000 or 6,000. Another cut that reflects the investment firm's large-cap products might reduce the set to 2,000 stocks—not a huge number, perhaps, but all firms have limited resources, especially of time and mind, that must be allocated well. These new disciplines can effectively screen and sort stocks based on financial returns and identify important changes that should consume analytical resources.

The PV methodologies can also help in the relative valuation of a large number of stocks. Key input decisions still must be made (consensus forecasts, proprietary data, etc.), and forecast accuracy should always be a source of humility, but these disciplines allow valuations to be made for a large universe and for multiple time periods.

Additionally, these disciplines can help us as analysts communicate better with our colleagues. If we were all so smart that we could do this analysis alone, we would not come to work. In fact, we come to work to make each other smarter, and the new methodologies provide a framework for the discourse that will make us smarter—a way for people to talk consistently and productively with each other and to collaborate across style and other boundaries. These PV disciplines do not eliminate conflict. We actually get smarter by having conflict—by not agreeing with each other and then by changing our minds. Unlike pure strife, which jeopardizes cognitive processes, conflict can expedite insight. These approaches are a rational way of dealing with productive conflict.

All decisions are ultimately based on judgment, but sometimes these new disciplines can identify deeply embedded prejudices and potentially critical problems that would otherwise be left implicit. For example, the statement "Food stocks never sell for more than eight times earnings" looks only at a P/E multiple with no way to relate that value to an EVA, a DCF, or even a DDM context. An analyst who looked at a company's expected revenues, use of corporate cash, and asset allocation and who concluded that a food stock was undervalued would have ammunition with which to argue against the multiples-based assertion. Unspoken beliefs are dangerous to the valuation process, and these new methodologies help make such beliefs explicit.

A new framework can also help run better "what-if" modeling. Given a specific company cost of capital, for example, the implied growth rate being assumed by the market can be isolated. Analysts who have focused solely on Intel's P/E have missed the importance of the durability and persistence of Intel's growth. Certain companies can reinvent product lines extremely well, and Intel has been such a company. For an analyst looking at Intel, the belief in the persistence of high returns may be entirely justified, not because of any multiple but because of the implied growth rate that derives from demonstrated results. Many U.S. companies with some of the best trademarks in the world are getting more and more of their growth from outside the United States. The new methodologies can be helpful in forcing the analyst to make at least a reasonable estimate of how long those trademarks, such as Coca-Cola or McDonalds or Disney, will continue to support above-average revenue and cash flow growth.

Implementation Problems

The biggest problem with implementing these new disciplines is that humans resist change, and institutional structures tend to reinforce that resistance. Because institutions are collections of individuals, getting institutions to think in different and new ways is very difficult. Few investment or brokerage firms have adopted these new methodologies as a consistent platform or even as part of a consistent platform. Rather, organizations tend to have islands of intensely loyal users of one or the other of the new approaches, which is probably the way these disciplines will gradually meld into the infrastructure of at least some buy-side firms. Many firms will not adopt these new methodologies at all; the apparent complexity of the new approaches is by itself enough to discourage some people, as is the lack of institutional will at the top of the organization.

Another difficulty is embedded in the sociology of the investment management business. A belief exists, certainly driven more by the media than by data, that some individual managers of large amounts of money consistently produce higher returns because of superior intelligence and intuition. If that belief were ever true, it would certainly not be true in these days when numerous money managers have vast amounts of money to manage. Statistics that track the number of managers who outperform the broader averages over some number of years indicate that such people are extremely rare. Because of the persistence of this belief, however, people hold on to the old view of the 1960s gunslinger cowboy manager who will shoot the lights out, knock out all the competition, and take all the fees. Given the historical reverence for individualism, this belief will probably die only slowly. Until it does die completely, these new methodologies, which obviously do not rely solely on the intelligence or charisma of individuals, will face resistance.

Finally, the new methodologies pose true technical problems that can be difficult to solve. For example, setting a discount rate in a country such as the United States can be mind-numbingly difficult, even though it appears straightforward. Trying to set a rate in markets outside the United States and trying to make cross-border rate comparisons can cause downright panic and despair. Comparing the Netherlands with Mexico with the United States, for example, is very difficult. The decision context must also be taken into account: Is the decision to allocate assets to Mexico, for example, or has the asset allocation already been made and is the decision simply to find the three cheapest, most liquid stocks in Mexico? In either case, what is the appropriate risk-free rate? Should the same rate be used for both decisions? These technical questions and problems do have a positive side, however; they force the analyst to focus on the right issues. From a competitive standpoint, addressing the issues that are at the forefront of the valuation process translates eventually into a competitive advantage; in the investment business, small incremental understanding can result in a very big payoff, and solving, or even simply discussing, these problems inevitably results in greater understanding.

Future Uses

The new methodologies will increasingly be delivered to buy-side organizations by Wall Street or will be adapted by sell-side firms and sold in a proprietary format. A trend is already beginning for Wall Street firms to intermediate some of these methodologies. For example, Goldman, Sachs & Company is developing its own EVA-based database of hundreds of companies and has indicated that its whole coverage universe will soon be available in an adapted EVA context. Credit Suisse First Boston also is using an EVA approach. More and more of the sell-side firms will have models in which users—the buy-side person, the client, for example—can enter growth rates and cash flow estimates and conduct their own analyses. This proliferation of models will be a boon to users but will also create a new problem: Whose EVA is to be trusted? Users will need enough knowledge of these methodologies to be intelligent consumers.

In the hands of dogmatists, these methodologies will fail. They provide a very useful valuation framework, but as with all methodologies, some people do, and will, get carried away by the pure intellectual elegance of these models. These tools are much better and more finely calibrated than those available in the past, but any tool, including these, used wrongly will still wreck the project. Very small errors in forecasting growth or in the discount rate can, and will, overwhelm the accuracy of other inputs and, more importantly, the insights gained about changes going on in an industry. Unfortunately, some people will believe that these new methodologies are so wonderfully systematic that they will tend to try to overuse them rather than to see them as simply one more heuristic, one more aid to discourse. The forecasts on which these methodologies are based are not good enough to provide surgical precision in making valuation decisions; rather, the aim should be to find the stocks that are substantially overvalued and substantially undervalued. If an analyst's fundamental insights are good and the inputs are right, that big mass of slightly mispriced stocks in the middle does not have much information content and is not worth thinking about. If these approaches permit us to be more correct than the market about the magnitude and direction of change, they will justify their use, even if they do not give us the precise value of a specific company.

Maybe the biggest evolutionary step for the new methodologies, and for the thinking they encourage, is that they are going global and will continue to do so. Communications technology and capital market sophistication have narrowed the spreads in global bonds in the past decade. The bond market is much more commoditized now than it was 5 or 10 years ago. The same is currently happening in global equity markets. Overseas, equity ownership is becoming more common: Governments are privatizing, more people are buying and selling stock, and the world outside the United States is becoming more equity literate. Corporate managements are listening to consultants who are spreading the message of EVA and kindred proprietary approaches around the world. Those investment professionals who have a high functional literacy rate in these new disciplines—who read the books and do the homework—will be able to interview managers better. Analysts interview managers in the United States more thoroughly—ask much more detailed questions—than they did just a few years ago simply because of increased insights into what truly drives business activity and the return on capital. The same process will happen outside the United States. The new methodologies create a common language and value set for companies within and outside the United States.

This global evolution comes with one caveat: Big regulatory hurdles must be overcome. In the Netherlands, for example, stock repurchase is not allowed. Much of the insight gained from these methodologies presupposes corporate management's ability to make free and unconstrained capital-allocation decisions; stock repurchase is one such decision. These methodologies will reach their full potential globally only when regulatory artifices are eliminated.

Finally, if these new methodologies work and are widely adopted, they will, of course, eventually be arbitraged out of the market, but such widespread adoption is not likely in the foreseeable future. More likely is the case of enthusiastic wholesale adoption on the part of a few firms and an informal adoption of the general philosophy and mindset on the part of many firms. These disciplines are merely tools; they may make capital markets a little more efficient over the next few decades, but the impact will be small and incremental.

Conclusion

The PV methodologies for equity valuation—DCF, EVA, and others—are commanding much more attention in investment circles, for good reason, than they have in the past. They are based on sound theory, have clear advantages over traditional valuation measures, and offer investment firms real potential benefits. They also, however, can be cumbersome compared with traditional measures, can pose implementation problems, and can threaten entrenched investment cultures. Their future widespread adoption, although likely, is not assured. In the end, good decisions will always be based on the use of good tools to form good judgments; these new methodologies are improved tools for better valuation judgments, resulting in clearer and more efficient decision making.

Question and Answer Session

Patrick O'Donnell
Joe Joseph[1]

Question: What methods did you consider when you designed your proprietary valuation model?

Joseph: Ours is a collection of a number of different PV approaches. We started with a very simple DCF approach; as the analysts got better at using it, it generated a lot more questions—some theoretical, some practical. We also looked at a number of commercial providers who used different variations of an EVA approach or a cash flow return on investment approach. So, we have used what we think is the best of literature and practice and adjusted for shortcomings that were database specific or the result of issues of market positioning. For example, the sales franchise method[2] has another form called "incremental threshold margin." We have been using that approach to separate how much of a company's value comes from existing businesses and new businesses.

O'Donnell: We decided early on that we would not wait for a utopian valuation formula. So, we just used what was available, hoping we would get better at the process as we used it. Indeed, the development process became iterative; every time somebody ran into something that was counterintuitive or posed an implementation problem, the discussion and solution made the model better.

---

[1]Joe Joseph, Mr. O'Donnell's colleague and deputy director of global equity research at Putnam Investment Management, joined him for the Question and Answer session.

[2]See Mr. Leibowitz's presentation, pp. 56–63.

Joseph: That process is still iterative. When we started applying the model in some of the newer emerging markets, such as Malaysia, many new issues arose: How long does it take for rapidly changing economic conditions to be reflected in a company's cost of capital? What is a company's competitive advantage period in rapidly developing economies? So, we are still learning and changing.

Question: Do your analysts make adjustments to a company's financial data?

Joseph: We began with the traditional EVA based on starting book value, so we had to make many accounting adjustments. We have moved away from that system to a complete cash-flow-based system, so we look at cash invested in the business and calculate the incremental return on that cash.

O'Donnell: We do not like book value. The knowledge that a company has a $1 billion modern factory has little, if any, information content from a valuation standpoint. We tend to look at everything in terms of the present value of the cash-on-cash returns, which is especially useful in evaluating companies outside the United States.

Question: Does the necessity of these accounting adjustments suggest that standards boards should rethink some of their positions?

Joseph: Today's financial statements are mixing up historical-based accounting and PV-based accounting, and the whole balance sheet is a "stew" of questionable numbers. All I ask for is a savings-type account: How much capital has management put in the business? How much capital has management taken out? Today's accounting statements do not let us get at that picture, which is why we have to spend hours adjusting those statements.

Question: EVA predicted correctly IBM Corporation's fall in the 1980s, but it missed its turn in the 1990s. Is EVA better at the top or at the bottom of a price move?

O'Donnell: Forecasts, not tools, predict moves. If you use a forward-looking discipline with the right forecasts, it will anticipate events. The hammer should not be blamed if the nail does not go in straight; it was the carpenter's fault. If you make the wrong forecast of sales and profits, you will miss the event, but that is the fault of the "carpenter," not the "tool." Therefore, the answer is that EVA is better when forecasts are better, whether at the top or bottom of a price move.

Question: How do you apply these new methodologies, especially EVA, to fast-growing small companies, such as venture-capital-financed or negative cash flow companies?

Joseph: With EVA, you are trying to forecast how long a company can earn relatively high incremental returns, how long it needs to invest, and what kind of a competitive advantage period it has. You can do that analysis just as easily for a fast-growing small company as for a slow-growing mature company. The more difficult issue is with venture-capital-type companies, where the success of a company is a function of whether a product succeeds or fails. In that case, you might have to rely more on certain types of option valuation techniques. In other words, if the product succeeds, then you are in the money, but if it does not, then you have lost your exercise price, which is the stock price today.

O'Donnell: Those of us who used DDMs 20 years ago remember how they always seemed to favor value stocks over growth stocks. The DDM was fairly neutral, but I think we as humans were reluctant to make the kinds of forecasts that justified the valuations for some of the fast-growing companies. There was a bias, but the bias was in us, not in the model. I think that in some technology companies, you do not need to go through an EVA-type process because the investment outcome is binary; that is, certain kinds of fast-growing technology companies will either succeed or fail. The detailed projections and concentrated analysis necessary to do EVA analysis correctly is probably not justifiable for a $200 million company.

Question: What role does beta play in your model?

Joseph: We do not use beta. The first problem with beta is that it is all backward looking. Second, companies that have stock prices that appreciated much faster than the market also have much higher betas, which does not mean that those companies are more risky. So, some of the beta logic simply does not work. What we try to do is identify the relative predictability of a company's cash flows. In other words, if we have a range of stocks, how predictable are the companies' cash flows? We do not care what the stock price does relative to the market. We are trying to assess relative predictability of the cash flows. So, we have a ranking mechanism that incorporates three factors that seem to us to affect cash flows: leverage, size, and industry (both within and across industries). We cannot precisely quantify the weights of these three factors, which is why we rely on the analyst's judgment.

O'Donnell: We tend to think like a lender. You trust me to manage your money. I turn around to the company and say, "I am going to give you this money, and here is the rate at which I am going to charge you rent on it, because here is what I think you can do in terms of paying me back." That process essentially describes how we set discount rates. If we think that the cash flow is very secure and very predictable, whatever the reported earnings, we expect that we will have to lower risk premiums relative to the other stocks.

Sales-Driven Franchise Value

Martin L. Leibowitz
Vice Chair and Chief Investment Officer
TIAA-CREF

The basic franchise value (FV) approach separates the value of a company into tangible value and franchise value, which are driven by current and future earnings. The sales-driven FV model recasts the two components in terms of current and future sales, resulting in an orientation that offers several advantages compared with traditional valuation approaches.

The ideas behind franchise-value (FV) analysis are not much different from those of many of the other new approaches to firm valuation. Many of these new approaches are grounded in present value (PV) and dividend discount model (DDM) frameworks. In one form or another, they all get at cash-flow analysis, and the FV approach is no exception. What is different is how the FV approach parses out some of the components that determine the value of the firm. This presentation begins with the basic FV approach, which was published in the monograph *Franchise Value and the Price/Earnings Ratio*, and continues with elaboration of the sales-driven FV approach, published in the monograph *Sales-Driven Franchise Value*.[1]

Basic Franchise-Value Approach

The basic idea of franchise value is that the value of a firm can be separated into two components, as shown in **Figure 1**. The first component is tangible value (TV), not tangible value in an accounting sense but the source of value that is embedded in the business that already exists—in the profits from current business. If no new fundamental investments are made, what will be the value of the business? The second component, the franchise value, addresses the question: If future new investments are made, what will be the value generated from those new investments? The FV turns out to be a function of profitability, the magnitude of

[1] Martin L. Leibowitz and Stanley Kogelman, *Franchise Value and the Price/Earnings Ratio* (Charlottesville, VA: The Research Foundation of the Institute of Chartered Financial Analysts, 1994); and Martin L. Leibowitz, *Sales-Driven Franchise Value* (Charlottesville, VA: The Research Foundation of the Institute of Chartered Financial Analysts, 1997).

future investment opportunities, and the capital costs associated with those opportunities.

The simple result, in terms of the total or intrinsic value of the firm, is the sum of the TV and the FV:

$$\text{Intrinsic value}, P = \text{Tangible value (TV)} + \text{Franchise value (FV)}.$$

Tangible Value. Tangible value is the capitalized profits from the current business. If one could look beyond simple earnings to come up with that elusive but critical number, the normalized earnings power, and then discount that number at the discount rate appropriate to the risk of the firm, the result would be the firm's TV. More specifically, the TV is the firm's book value times the normalized current return on equity (ROE) divided by an appropriate capitalization rate:

$$
\begin{aligned}
\text{TV} &= \text{Capitalized profit from current business} \\
&= \frac{\text{Normalized current earnings}, E}{\text{Discount rate}, k} \\
&= \frac{(\text{Normalized current ROE}, r) \times (\text{Book value}, B)}{k} \\
&= \frac{rB}{k}.
\end{aligned}
$$

In other words, the TV is the rate of return on the existing business times the book value divided by the discount rate; this expression for TV assumes that a stream of earnings has been created from the current business that will essentially go on forever.

Franchise Value. The key measure in FV is the return above and beyond the cost of capital, and the key question is how a company can extract that return. The answer is that the company has to have something special. If a company simply makes a

Figure 1. Franchise-Value Approach

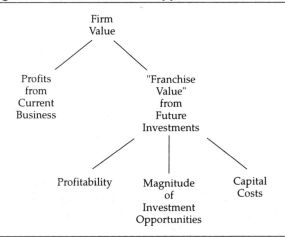

regular investment, that company should earn the cost of capital for the particular risk it is taking. To be able to get any FV at all, investing is not enough; the company has to invest and get an excess return. What creates that extra return? Perhaps the company has a better distribution system than its competitors. Perhaps the company has a patent or licensing arrangement. The company must have something special that is not given to just anyone who happens to have available capital. That something is a franchise.

A firm's FV consists of three factors: the present value of future investment opportunities, a normalized excess ROE, and a capitalization factor.

$$FV = \text{Capitalized future profits above and beyond the cost of capital}$$

$$= (\text{Present value of future opportunities, PVop, to invest at new ROE, } R)$$
$$\times (\text{Normalized excess ROE, } R - k)$$
$$\times (\text{Capitalization factor, } 1/k)$$

$$= PVop \times \left(\frac{R-k}{k}\right).$$

The first factor is the PV of the firm's future investment opportunities: how much fresh money the firm can put usefully to work. That PV is multiplied by the second factor, $R - k$, which is the return that will be received in excess of the cost of the capital. Essentially, one can envision a stream of opportunities that is growing over time. The firm is investing in each of those opportunities and creating a series of future earnings from each of those investments. It can be shown that this product reduces the excess earnings to an equivalent constant payment that would be received annually in perpetuity. This annual payment is then multiplied by the capitalization factor, $1/k$, to provide a simple present value equivalent of the far more complex actual stream of excess profits.

Estimating PVop is admittedly difficult; to be tractable, it must be put into a simpler framework.

One approach is to view it as a growth factor. Essentially, the opportunities for investing in the future, which create the future book of business in PV terms, correspond to some factor, G, times the current book value, B:

$$PVop \equiv \text{Growth factor} \times \text{Book value}$$
$$= G \times B.$$

For example, with perpetual growth at a constant rate g, the growth factor G takes on the form

$$G = \frac{g}{k-g}.$$

The growth factor approach is quite general, however, and can represent the present value of virtually any pattern of growth, no matter how complex. With this growth factor in hand, the FV calculation becomes simpler: FV is the growth factor times the current book value times the excess earnings capability factor:

$$FV = G \times B \times \left(\frac{R-k}{k}\right).$$

The P/E in Franchise-Value Terms. Franchise-value theory actually began by trying to understand P/E from an analytical point of view. Academic literature tends to focus on PV—most of the Modigliani and Miller work was done in terms of PV—and relatively few academic studies focus directly on P/E. In the world of practice, however, P/E dominates. People use, and misuse, P/E every day in every way. FV provides a way of looking at P/E in terms of the discount rate, the ROE on new investments, the ROE on old investments, and the growth factor, which represents the range of opportunities for such new investments.

A deeper understanding of the pervasive P/E can be obtained by parsing out the value sources using the FV framework. The first step is to express the P/E in terms of the TV and the FV:

$$P/E = \frac{TV + FV}{E}.$$

TV is the normalized earnings divided by the discount rate. So, when TV is divided by the earnings, E, the result is 1 over the discount rate:

$$\frac{TV}{E} = \frac{1}{k}.$$

Going through the same division process for the FV term results in the excess earnings factor times the growth factor times a book-to-earnings ratio:

$$\frac{FV}{E} = \left(\frac{R-k}{k}\right) \times G \times \frac{B}{E}.$$

Because earnings can be expressed as the current (normalized) ROE, r, times the book value, B,

$$E = rB.$$

FV divided by earnings can then be expressed as

$$\frac{FV}{E} = \left(\frac{R-k}{k}\right) \times G \times \frac{1}{r}$$
$$= \left(\frac{R-k}{rk}\right) \times G.$$

Bringing these results together enables the P/E to be expressed as

$$P/E = \frac{1}{k} + \left(\frac{R-k}{rk}\right) \times G.$$

The first term is the reciprocal of the discount rate, $1/k$. The factor $(R-k)/rk$, which we call the "franchise factor," represents the P/E increment generated by each present value dollar of new investment opportunities. The growth factor, G, reflects the present value magnitude of projected investment opportunities per dollar of current book value.

This model enables investors to distinguish the return that they are earning on the existing book of business, r, from the return that they will get on their new business opportunities, R. This distinction is important for several reasons. The return on the old book of business may be distorted by all kinds of accounting considerations as well as many historical legacies; it certainly does not represent the fact that investors can *freely* choose their new investment opportunities and thus should be able, under fairly general circumstances, to obtain a higher ROE on those investments. That is, in general, R should be bigger than r.

Sales-Driven Franchise Approach

The sales-driven franchise approach, an elaboration of FV, arose from a consideration of international investing. One can envision a world where globalization is taken to its ultimate extreme. This world does not yet exist, and probably never will, but companies in such a world could manufacture products anywhere, which would create an equalization of the cost of goods manufactured. The real issue would then be what kind of sales these companies can generate and at what profit margins, both in terms of their current business and their future business. This idea prompted changing the basic driving variables in the FV framework from earnings to sales. Thus, the sales-driven approach has the same kind of breakdown—current business versus future opportunities—as the original FV approach, but as shown in **Figure 2**, the focus is now on the profit margin on sales and the magnitude of the future sales relative to current sales, with capital costs still an integral part of the formulation.

The focus on sales makes sense in several ways. At a basic level, sales are more fundamental than earnings to a company's true value. Sales are less vulnerable to accounting distortions, and to a large

Figure 2. Sales-Driven Franchise Approach

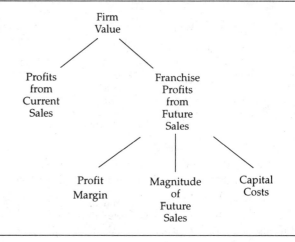

extent, companies in the same business can be compared in terms of their sales and margins on a much more direct basis. So, there are many advantages to looking at companies in terms of their current sales, the opportunity for generating future sales, and the current and future margins that can be extracted from those sales.

Tangible Value in Sales Terms. Translating TV, the current business term, into a sales-driven type of variable is simple. The net profit margin times the normalized current sales corresponds to the normalized earnings. Applying the same discount rate results in the sales-driven TV:

$$TV = \frac{E}{k}$$
$$= \frac{(\text{Profit margin}, m) \times (\text{Normalized current sales}, S)}{k}$$
$$= \frac{m \times S}{k}.$$

Franchise Value in Sales Terms. In the sales-driven context, FV retains the basic idea of future investments but the focus is the future new sales—sales not currently being generated. What is important is the earnings from the future sales that are achieved above and beyond the cost of capital:

$$FV = \text{Capitalized future profits above and beyond the cost of capital}$$

$$= (\text{Present value of future sales derived from new investments, } PVsls)$$
$$\times [(\text{Profit margin on future new sales, } m')$$
$$- (\text{Capital costs to generate each dollar of future new sales, } c')]$$

$$= PVsls \times (m' - c').$$

The PV of future new sales, PVsls, is multiplied by the profit margin, m', on every one of those new (indicated by the prime) sales dollars. Then the capi-

Table 1. Sales Growth Factor, *G'*

	Growth Rate				
Years of Growth	6 Percent	8 Percent	12 Percent	16 Percent	18 Percent
5	0.24	0.33	0.54	0.77	0.89
10	0.42	0.61	1.07	1.68	2.06
20	0.67	1.03	2.14	4.07	5.52
30	0.81	1.32	3.21	7.46	11.36
Infinity	1.00	2.00	—	—	—

Note: Assumes growth over each year leads to higher rate of annual sales at beginning of next year, resulting in higher sales and earnings receipts at the end of the next year.

tal cost, c', incurred to generate each dollar of new (again indicated by the prime) sales is subtracted.

As was the case for PVop in the former FV case, a growth factor, G', can be multiplied by the PV of current sales to estimate PVsls. With this sales growth factor introduced, the PV of future sales derived from new investments becomes

PVsls ≡ (Sales growth factor, G') × (Present value of sales from current business)

$$= G' \times (\text{Normalized current annual sales, } S) \times (\text{Capitalization factor, } 1/k)$$

$$= G' \times S \times \left(\frac{1}{k}\right).$$

The FV then becomes

$$FV = G' \times \left(\frac{S}{k}\right) \times (m' - c').$$

The sales growth factor admittedly says nothing about how sales are developed, whether growth is smooth or erratic, or whether growth peaks or is delayed for a long period. But one of the great features of the PV of future sales or PV of future earnings approaches is that any kind of growth pattern, no matter how erratic, can be discounted back to the PV. All growth patterns, if they have the same PV, will have the same impact on the valuation of the firm, so a whole host of different types of evolutionary patterns for the growth of the firm can be used. **Table 1** provides a simple model of constant growth for a discount rate of 12 percent: If the firm's sales grow at 8 percent for 10 years, the growth factor is 0.61. If sales grow *forever* at 8 percent, the growth factor is 2.00. (For this special case of the infinite horizon, we have $G = g/k - g = 8/12 - 8 = 2.00$.) Growth rates higher than the discount rate over an infinite horizon would yield an infinite value for the sales growth factor, which is not meaningful. Using time horizons with reasonable growth rates is important.[2]

Sales-Driven FV Model

Having TV and FV in sales terms allows the two to be combined and shows both to be related to a com-

---

[2] For further discussion and derivation of the sales growth factor, see Leibowitz, *Sales-Driven Franchise Value*.

mon variable—the current annual rate of sales, S:

$$P = TV + FV$$

$$= \frac{m \times S}{k} + (m' - c') \times G' \times \left(\frac{S}{k}\right).$$

Factoring out S produces

$$P = S\left[\frac{m}{k} + \left(\frac{m' - c'}{k}\right) \times G'\right].$$

Capital Cost of Future Sales. The capital cost from each dollar of future sales, c', bears discussion, because it is not an intuitive figure. The key is to use the traditional turnover rate (T'), which is the annual sales generated from each dollar of new investment. So, for example, if T' equals 3, a stream of $3 of annual sales is generated for every $1 of investment today. Because this model is intended to be sales driven, a better question is: If $3 of new sales can be generated, how much of an investment needs to be made now? The answer would be $1. The reciprocal of the turnover rate ($1/T'$) shows that the capital required to generate $1 of new annual sales is just 33 cents. Because this capital is expended at the outset and what is really needed is the capital cost for each year, the capital cost today has to be multiplied by the cost of capital for each year. So, the *annual* cost of new capital required to generate $1 of new annual sales is the capital cost factor, k, times the reciprocal of T'— that is, $k \times 1/T'$. We can now see that this formulation corresponds to a more intuitive way to express c', the capital cost for each dollar of new sales.

Franchise Margin. The key component in the sales-driven model turns out to be the franchise margin, fm': the ability to extract from each dollar of future sales a profit margin that exceeds the cost of capital. The fm' is just $m' - c'$, or the difference between the earnings generated for each $1 of new sales and the cost of capital associated with that dollar of sales. As such, the franchise margin is the net payoff to today's shareholders for each $1 of new sales generated:

fm' ≡ Profit per dollar of new sales above and beyond the cost of required capital

$$= m' - c'$$

$$= m' - \frac{k}{T'}.$$

The franchise margin, fm', can also serve as a gauge of the firm's profitability relative to that of prospective "commodity competitors." Suppose some entrepreneur wants to enter the company's business and that entrepreneur can enjoy roughly the same production and capital costs as the company. If the entrepreneur can generate a fm' of zero plus some small incremental return, it has covered its cost of capital and can have some profit. It will then have an incentive to enter the business. So, in a certain sense, a fm' of zero would be the point at which capital would start to be drawn into this business, and one could assume that, barring special considerations, this is the point at which any given company would start to feel pressures on its margin. If a company has a fm' greater than zero, it will start to attract new investors, new enterprises, new companies into its business, barring other types of barriers to entry.

Thus, if a company has a sustainable fm' of 5 percent in a particular product line, that value of fm' is in some ways a gauge of its pricing power—its ability to extract a market price that is above and beyond the price at which a serious competitor could enter the market. The idea of a firm's pricing power is critical. In company analysis, it is important to note the special factors—the patents, the distribution channels, the skilled personnel and/or the organizational advantages—that enable a company to extract a positive franchise margin on an ongoing basis. Investors need to know what enables a company to defend against the encroachment of potential "phantom" competitors who would be quite happy to earn slightly more than a fm' of zero.

A company's fm' can also be used to relate the sales turnover rate and the annual cost of capital for each $1 of sales, as shown in **Figure 3**. As the sales turnover goes up, obviously, capital is used more efficiently and the c' line follows a downward sloping path. The money investors earn in terms of net value is given by the profit margin less the cost of capital, so the difference between the c' curve and the horizontal m' line is the fm'. Thus, one can see that fm' is very sensitive to sales turnover at the low end of sales turnover rates but then is relatively insensitive at the high end of sales turnover rates.

Franchise Margin Model. The fm' allows for the construction of a simple formulation for the intrinsic value of a company. Previously, the intrinsic value was written as

$$P = S\left[\frac{m}{k} + \left(\frac{m'-c'}{k}\right)G'\right].$$

Using the expression $c' = k/T'$ gives the following:

$$P = S\left[\frac{m}{k} + \frac{1}{k}\left(m' - \frac{k}{T'}\right)G'\right].$$

By factoring out and using fm', the franchise margin, for $m' - k/T'$, the intrinsic value becomes

$$P = S\left[\frac{m}{k} + \frac{fm'}{k}G'\right].$$

Therefore, a company's intrinsic value is its current annualized sales rate times an expression that consists of its current margin divided by the discount rate plus the fm' on new business divided by the discount rate times the growth factor of new sales.

Valuation Ratios Using the Franchise Margin Model. The expression for firm value just given leads to alternate ways of representing the familiar valuation ratios, such as price to sales and price to earnings:

$$P/S = \frac{m}{k} + \frac{fm'}{k}G'$$

$$P/E = \frac{1}{m}(P/S)$$

$$= \frac{1}{k} + \frac{fm'}{mk}G'.$$

This sales-driven P/E formulation has the same general form as the earlier "investment-driven" expression. The P/E increment per unit growth is now given by fm'/mk, which is roughly equivalent to the investment-driven franchise factor.

Example of Franchise Margin Model. A company with current sales of $300 million a year, a book value of $100 million (which corresponds to a current turnover rate of 3), a margin of 6 percent, and a cost of capital of 12 percent will have the following TV:

$$TV = \frac{m \times S}{k}$$

$$= \frac{0.06 \times \$300\text{ million}}{0.12}$$

$$= \$150\text{ million.}$$

Figure 3. The Franchise Margin: Annual Capital Cost as a Percentage of Sales, c', versus Sales Turnover Rate, T'

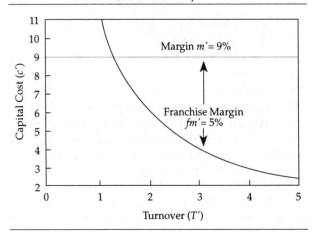

If the future profit margin rate is 9 percent and the turnover rate is essentially the same as on the current book of business, the *fm'* calculation is

$$fm' = m' - \frac{k}{T'}$$

$$= 0.09 - \frac{0.12}{3}$$

$$= 0.05.$$

Assuming perpetual growth at 8 percent produces a sales growth factor of 2. FV then becomes

$$G' = 2.00;$$

$$FV = \frac{fm'}{k} \times G' \times S$$

$$= \frac{0.05}{0.12} \times 2 \times \$300 \text{ million}$$

$$= \$250 \text{ million.}$$

Total firm value is as follows:

$$P = TV + FV$$

$$= \$150 \text{ million} + \$250 \text{ million}$$

$$= \$400 \text{ million.}$$

The P/S and P/E, respectively, are

$$P/S = \frac{400}{300} = 1.33;$$

$$P/E = \frac{1}{m}(P/S) = \frac{1.33}{0.06} = 22.22.$$

This example can be extended to illustrate the results of different assumptions about the magnitude of *fm'*. **Figure 4** illustrates perpetual growth with sustained margins. The sales start off at a current level of $300 million and have a profit margin, *m*, of 6 percent and a franchise margin, *fm*, on *current sales* of 2 percent (*fm* = 0.06 − 0.12/3). These sales go on

Figure 4.   Perpetual Growth with Sustained Margins

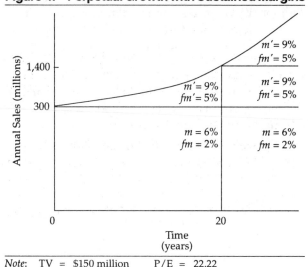

Note: TV = $150 million   P/E = 22.22
         FV = $250 million   P/S =   1.33
         P   = $400 million   P/B =   4.00

essentially forever at this $300 million level, which is the TV component. The future sales are growing smoothly at a rate of 8 percent annually, and those future sales have a profit margin, *m'*, of 9 percent and a franchise margin of future sales, *fm'*, of 5 percent.

At the 20th year, the assumption of continual 8 percent sales growth generates some pretty remarkable numbers. A growth factor of 2 times seems modest, but sales would have to rise from $300 million annually today to $1.4 billion annually in 20 years and would have to continue growing. Not only is the assumption that the sales continue to grow, but the assumption is also that sales continue to grow at the same high level of profitability. In addition, the model assumes that no competitors come in to try to take this market away or to try to force lower pricing.

Suppose now that everything happens as just described up until the 20th year, but at the 20th year, the company hits that $1.4 billion in annual sales and finds itself at the edge of a cliff, as shown in **Figure 5**. The cliff can take two forms, both of which turn out to be mathematically identical. In the first form, sales flatten at the $1.4 billion level, but the company con-

Figure 5.   Twenty-Year Franchise Horizon

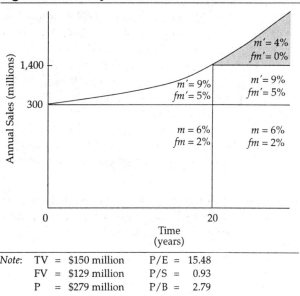

Note: TV = $150 million   P/E = 15.48
         FV = $129 million   P/S =   0.93
         P   = $279 million   P/B =   2.79

tinues to dominate the market so that nothing happens to profit margins. The company still gets the 9 percent on all sales that were initiated after the outset—all sales above and beyond the original $300 million—but the company does not enjoy any sales growth beyond the $1.4 billion. In the second form of the cliff, sales continue to grow at 8 percent forever. The company still manages to get more and more growth, but competitors have entered the market looking for returns just above their cost of capital, so the original company has to provide competitive pricing. The company's profit margin of 9 percent on all new sales beyond the $1.4 billion level is driven down to 4 percent. Therefore, the franchise margin declines to zero, and these future sales thus have no value for the shareholders. This situation can be shown to be mathematically equivalent to the first form of the cliff, where the sales actually leveled off. (This finding, which is far from obvious, is shown in *Sales-Driven Franchise Value.*) These "cliff scenarios" do not affect TV, which is based on the sales of $300 million. They do, however, bring FV down—from what had been $250 million to now $129 million. Therefore, the value of the firm goes down from $400 million to $279 million, and P/E goes down from 22 to roughly 15.5.

Once this line of analysis is established, even more extreme cases can be analyzed. If competition kicks in at the 20th year in a serious way and squeezes margins on any new sales beyond that point, why should it not squeeze margins on sales already achieved to that point? After all, why should only the incremental sales be affected, especially if this is a single product line? **Figure 6** shows what happens to the company if margins are squeezed on all sales

---

Figure 6. New Sales Margin Collapse at Horizon

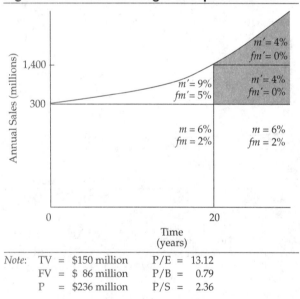

Note: TV = $150 million   P/E = 13.12
       FV = $ 86 million   P/B = 0.79
       P = $236 million   P/S = 2.36

---

above $300 million—the value of the firm drops further, to $236 million, with a corresponding decrease in the valuation ratios.

The most extreme case is a margin squeeze on all sales, even the initial level of $300 million, caused by competitors who are willing to compete on all sales for a *fm'* that is only slightly above zero. **Figure 7** shows that the value of the firm and the various ratios

Figure 7. Total Margin Collapse at Horizon

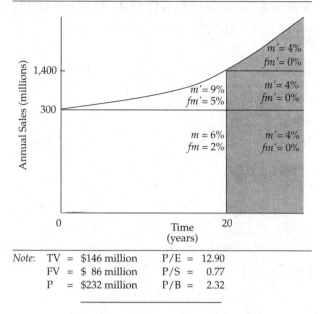

Note: TV = $146 million   P/E = 12.90
       FV = $ 86 million   P/S = 0.77
       P = $232 million   P/B = 2.32

---

continue to decline, although it may be some small comfort that the marginal damage over and above that suffered in Figure 6 is fairly small.

Conclusion

Capital is not a scarce resource in the current business environment. Generating internal capital will not allow a company to fend off competitors. If a company's competitor has a better patent or any other demonstrably better competitive feature, it can get capital. So, what investors need is a way of identifying something beyond just the availability of capital in a global marketplace that enables a company to retain pricing power and to extract a franchise margin. The original investment-driven FV approach has its own virtues, but a sales-driven type of orientation offers additional advantages. The sales-driven approach

- is a better fit for multinational companies, because the production costs can ultimately be equilibrated,
- uses sales and margin parameters, which are more intuitive and more directly estimable for most investors than ROE components,
- places market opportunities front and center as the primary drivers of investment activity and value creation,
- underscores the role of pricing power as a source for profit,
- relates sales turnover, which is a fairly stable input and a key underpinning of ROE, and capital costs to franchise opportunity, and
- explicitly deals with the point at which competitive pressures come into play and what impact they can have on future margins.

Question and Answer Session

Martin L. Leibowitz

Question: How does the sales-driven FV approach differ from an economic value added (EVA) approach?

Leibowitz: A fundamental PV type of analysis underlies all these approaches. It is a question of how you parse out the components of value and which components you emphasize. EVA does a remarkable job of digging into the accounting measures and showing how they relate to value. From that point forward, in terms of analyzing how the various sources of value constitute the total value of the firm, I think all these measures have to end up in the same place: They have to be useful to the analyst. I think these approaches are quite consistent.

Question: Is the FV approach best used by money managers or as an internal capital-allocation tool for a company?

Leibowitz: We have developed it more as a tool for security analysis than for corporate analysis, although I think they coincide in their final results. Some form of the concept of franchise value, and certainly sales-driven franchise value, should be a central concept in corporate planning.

Question: The sales-driven FV model started out with international companies in mind, but can it also be used for domestic companies?

Leibowitz: Yes, certainly. I think you will find the most new insights from this approach in those cases in which sales are starting to come under competitive pressures and you want to assess the effects of those pressures over time. This analysis requires estimating the period over which margin levels can be sustained, as well as the degree of margin erosion that then occurs. The various growth models presented in *Sales-Driven Franchise Value* should be helpful in this valuation process.

Question: Does a company's capital structure—how the company finances its sales growth—affect your approach?

Leibowitz: The model illustrated in this presentation assumes total equity funding. Incorporating debt financing is fairly straightforward, but I think it is unnecessarily complicated for presentation purposes. The basic change in orientation involves looking at enterprise value in a free cash flow format, or through operating flows less financing flows, to reflect the particular form of financing.

Question: Does the tangible book value approach imply a perpetuity?

Leibowitz: For the sake of simplicity, I assumed normalized streams that go out forever as the basis for tangible value. The concept is much more general than

that. The real question in tangible value is what is the value of the business if it does not make any new investments (i.e., if it does not have to incur any future financing). What is the value of that business right now? In actuality, the current business will obviously not generate a perpetual earnings stream. The actual profits might rise for a certain period, but they will almost surely begin to erode at some point. In practice, it may be no simple task to estimate the path of earnings derived from the current business under the assumption of no further investment. But once this literal earnings stream is estimated, its present value can be determined. Our formulation of the tangible value uses the idealized model of a perpetual "normalized" earnings stream that is the present value equivalent of the more complex literal path of earnings. This present value equivalence can always be found, and it is simply a more mathematically tractable way of representing a complex reality.

Question: Do you use the FV approach in the portfolio you manage?

Leibowitz: Yes, but carefully. I think it is very important that one be eclectic and use a wide variety of different fundamental approaches. Specific tools are helpful in illuminating different aspects of the investment challenge.

Self-Evaluation Examination

1. Empirical research indicates that recommendations from analysts on the *Institutional Investor* All-America Research Team affect stock prices more than do other analysts' recommendations in the case of which of the following large earnings forecast revisions?
   A. Both upward and downward.
   B. Upward but not downward.
   C. Downward but not upward.
   D. Neither upward nor downward.

2. Based on a review of empirical evidence about the usefulness of Wall Street research, Timura concludes that investors:
   A. Cannot earn abnormal returns by trading on the basis of changes in analysts' investment advice.
   B. Can earn abnormal returns by trading in the opposite direction of changes in analysts' investment advice.
   C. Can earn abnormal returns by trading in the direction of changes in analysts' investment advice.
   D. Cannot execute the trades that would be required to respond to changes in analysts' investment advice.

3. Investors can use Wall Street research to discern market expectations on the basis of:
   I. Industry analysis.
   II. Financial statement information.
   III. Historical company analysis.
   A. I and II only.
   B. I and III only.
   C. II and III only.
   D. I, II, and III.

4. Creative intelligence gathering addresses the typical need for an investor to:
   I. Make an investment decision immediately.
   II. Enhance understanding in the long term.
   III. Generate new ideas for further research.
   A. II only.
   B. III only.
   C. II and III only.
   D. I, II, and III.

5. According to Dolliver, when conducting creative intelligence gathering for information about a company, making effective use of contact time specifically includes:
   A. Remembering a source's potential biases.
   B. Using examples of similar companies in similar situations.
   C. Positing a null hypothesis about the company for research purposes.
   D. Contacting regulatory officials or lobbyists who are familiar with the company.

6. Creative intelligence gathering is most accurately characterized as being:
   I. Conducted exclusively on a person-to-person basis.
   II. Based on the unique use of readily available information.
   III. Focused outside the normal research channels.
   A. I only.
   B. III only.
   C. I and II only.
   D. I, II, and II.

7. As part of his left-brain analysis, Speece includes which of the following as examples of "normal" unusual accounting items?
   I. Working capital management.
   II. Allowance for doubtful accounts.
   III. Restructuring charges.
   IV. Pension plan investment assumptions.
   A. I and II only.
   B. II and IV only.
   C. III and IV only.
   D. I, II, III, and IV.

8. Proxies can be a valuable part of right-brain analysis by providing insights into a company's:
   I. Composition of management.
   II. Compensation system.
   III. Party of interest transactions.
   IV. Ownership structure.
   A. I only.
   B. IV only.
   C. II and IV only.
   D. I, II, III, and IV.

9. The most useful tool for identifying the emotional extremes reflected by management and investors is the:
   A. Proxy.
   B. Conference call.
   C. Record of changes in company ownership.
   D. Existence and nature of party of interest transactions.

10. When Martin used four traditional equity valuation methods to screen a stock universe, he found that portfolios *generally* exhibiting the highest value, return on equity, and growth are those portfolios formed on the basis of the:
    A. Price-to-earnings ratio.
    B. Price-to-sales ratio.
    C. Price-to-book ratio.
    D. Dividend discount model.

11. Which of the following relationships exists between P/Es, growth rates, and discount rates? P/Es:
    A. Increase as growth rates increase but decrease as discount rates increase.
    B. Increase as growth rates increase and increase as discount rates decrease.
    C. Decrease as growth rates increase but increase as discount rates increase.
    D. Are not systematically related to either growth rates or discount rates.

12. Which of the following statements about price-implied growth and growth duration are accurate?
    I. *Price-implied growth* is used to justify the spread between the P/E of an individual stock and the P/E of an index.
    II. *Growth duration* is used to justify the current P/E of a company or group of companies.
    A. I only.
    B. II only.
    C. Both I and II.
    D. Neither I nor II.

13. Ohlson defines the value of a company as the:
    A. Present value of expected free cash flows, net of capital expenditures, less net financial obligations.
    B. Present value of expected free cash flows, including capital expenditures, less net financial obligations.
    C. Present value of expected free cash flows, net of capital expenditures, plus net financial obligations.
    D. Present value of expected free cash flows, including capital expenditures, plus net financial obligations.

14. Which of the following problems are encountered in analyzing earnings based on generally accepted accounting principles?
    I. Discount rates.
    II. Continuing values.
    III. Restructuring charges.
    IV. Pension and postretirement expenses.
    A. I and II only.
    B. III and IV only.
    C. II, III, and IV only.
    D. I, II, III, and IV.

15. What is the correct sequence of steps in applying free cash flow analysis to stock valuation?
    I. Calculate levered return on equity.
    II. Relate return on equity to risk.
    III. Infer expected return on the unlevered company.
    IV. Estimate free cash flow.
    V. Estimate anticipated growth in free cash flow.
    A. I, II, III, IV, V.
    B. III, I, II, IV, V.
    C. III, IV, V, I, II.
    D. IV, V, III, I, II.

16. To gain insight into a company's capital efficiency, Jackson advocates comparing that company's return on invested capital with its:
    A. Total asset base.
    B. Net operating profit after taxes.
    C. Net working capital.
    D. Weighted-average cost of capital.

17. Economic value added analysis can be used to determine whether a company's:
    I. High-return businesses subsidize low-return businesses.
    II. Geographical operations add value to the company.
    III. Business segments create value for the company.
    A. I and II only.
    B. I and III only.
    C. II and III only.
    D. I, II, and III.

18. Using economic value added analysis to compare two business units' returns and the amounts of capital invested in each unit is an example of assessing:
    A. Segment performance.
    B. Subsidization.
    C. Capital efficiency.
    D. Fair value.

19. The present value approaches to equity valuation all share a:
    I. Focus on the company's cost of capital.
    II. Rejection of GAAP-based accounting measures.
    III. Reliance on risk adjustment factors.
    A. I and II only.
    B. I and III only.
    C. II and III only.
    D. I, II, and III.

20. According to O'Donnell, all of the following are advantages of present value methodologies for equity valuation *except* that such methodologies:
    A. Provide a consistent and clear framework for valuation.
    B. Use consistent financial inputs.
    C. Are appropriate for all investment approaches.
    D. Can explicitly link forecasted returns and stock prices.

21. Which of the following are potential benefits of present value methodologies for equity valuation?
    I. Identify embedded prejudices.
    II. Improve quality of communication.
    III. Screen large stock universes.
    IV. Allow relative stock valuations.
    A. IV only.
    B. I and II only.
    C. III and IV only.
    D. I, II, III, and IV.

22. The total, or intrinsic, value of the company is best expressed as that company's:
    A. Tangible value less franchise value.
    B. Franchise value less tangible value.
    C. Tangible value plus franchise value.
    D. Franchise value times tangible value.

23. Which of the following best describes the tangible value and/or franchise value of a company?
    A. Tangible value is the capitalized profit from current business, and franchise value is the capitalized future profits in excess of the company's cost of capital.
    B. Franchise value is the capitalized profit from current business, and tangible value is the capitalized future profits in excess of the company's cost of capital.
    C. Tangible value is normalized excess return on equity multiplied by a capitalization factor.
    D. Franchise value is normalized current earnings multiplied by a capitalization factor.

24. Leibowitz contends that the key component in the sales-driven franchise-value model is the:
    A. Capital cost of future sales.
    B. Franchise margin.
    C. Present value of future sales.
    D. Profit margin on normalized current sales.

Self-Evaluation Answers

1. B. Timura cites research by Stickel, who studied patterns of stock returns following earnings revisions from the All-America Research Team and other analysts. He concluded that those patterns differed between the two groups in the case of upward revisions but not in the case of downward revisions.

2. C. The evidence indicates that, although analysts may be slow to react and prone to overreact to new earnings information, investors can earn abnormal returns by trading in the direction recommended by analysts.

3. D. Timura contends that investors should be able to use Wall Street information in all three ways, as well as to provide a sounding board for new ideas and to help discern market expectations.

4. D. Dolliver believes that creative intelligence gathering addresses the typical information needs of both analysts and investors—needs that may take any one of the three forms indicated.

5. A. Making effective use of contact time includes remembering a source's biases, as well as defining the information needed, being straightforward, identifying other sources, expressing thanks, and avoiding a crisis context.

6. B. Dolliver explains that many creative intelligence-gathering activities center on physical information sources (libraries, the Internet) rather than people, and almost by definition, creative intelligence gathering must go beyond readily available information and normal channels.

7. A. Restructuring charges and pension plan investment assumptions are separate aspects of the quality of earnings rather than examples of "normal" unusual accounting items.

8. D. Speece discusses how proxies can provide important information about all four company characteristics.

9. B. Speece contends that listening to the tone of a conference call allows analysts to go beyond numbers to underlying emotional indicators revealed by both management and other analysts, particularly when the company is at a potential turning point.

10. D. The portfolio formed by the dividend discount model had the highest price-to-earnings, price-to-sales, and price-to-book ratios; highest return on equity; and highest 10-year growth rate.

11. B. Martin demonstrates that P/Es are exponentially related to growth and discount rates, increasing as growth rates increase and/or as discount rates decrease.

12. D. Martin's discussion of the two concepts indicates that the two statements are exactly reversed.

13. A. The intrinsic value of a company's equity equals the present value of expected free cash flows, net of capital expenditures, minus the company's net financial obligations.

14. B. According to Ohlson, discount rates and continuing values are examples of the practical questions that must be addressed in taking a free cash flow approach to valuation.

15. D. Ohlson details a valuation process that begins with estimating current free cash flow and concludes with relating return to risk by means of an explicit risk adjustment.

16. D. Comparing a company's return on invested capital with its weighted-average cost of capital for a given period can provide insight into that company's capital efficiency, which suggests how well that company's stock will perform.

17. D. Jackson believes that economic value added analysis can be used to answer all three questions, as well as whether incremental returns exceed capital costs, whether capital is used efficiently, and which stocks are likely to outperform the market.

18. B. Jackson describes how economic value added analysis can be used to determine the extent to which high-return business units are subsidizing low-return business units.

19. D. All three characteristics are what O'Donnell terms "commonalities" of present-value-based disciplines.

20. C. One of the disadvantages of present value methodologies is that they are *not* appropriate for all investment approaches. For instance, they are useless for momentum, sector rotation, and high-growth, small cap strategies.

21. D. O'Donnell contends that present value methodologies offer investment firms all four potential benefits.

22. C. Leibowitz shows that a company's total, or intrinsic, value is the sum of that company's tangible value and franchise value.

23. A. Leibowitz distinguishes between the two components of a company's total value: Tangible value derives from current business, and franchise value derives from future investments.

24. B. The most important component in the sales-driven franchise-value model is the franchise margin, which measures the ability to extract from each dollar of future sales a profit margin that exceeds the cost of capital.

Selected Publications

AIMR

AIMR Performance Presentation Standards Handbook, 2nd edition, 1997

Asian Equity Investing, 1998

Deregulation of the Electric Utility Industry, 1997

Economic Analysis for Investment Professionals, 1997

Finding Reality in Reported Earnings, 1997
Jan R. Squires, CFA, *Editor*

Global Bond Management, 1997
Jan R. Squires, CFA, *Editor*

Implementing Global Equity Strategy: Spotlight on Asia, 1997

Investing in Small-Cap and Microcap Securities, 1997

Investing Worldwide VIII: Developments in Global Portfolio Management, 1997

Managing Currency Risk, 1997

Standards of Practice Casebook, 1996

Standards of Practice Handbook, 7th edition, 1996

Research Foundation

Blockholdings of Investment Professionals
by Sanjai Bhagat, Bernard S. Black, and Margaret M. Blair

Company Performance and Measures of Value Added
by Pamela P. Peterson, CFA, and David R. Peterson

Controlling Misfit Risk in Multiple-Manager Investment Programs
by Jeffery V. Bailey, CFA, and David E. Tierney

Country Risk in Global Financial Management
by Claude B. Erb, CFA, Campbell R. Harvey, and Tadas E. Viskanta

Economic Foundations of Capital Market Returns
by Brian D. Singer, CFA, and Kevin Terhaar, CFA

Initial Dividends and Implications for Investors
by James W. Wansley, CFA, William R. Lane, CFA, and Phillip R. Daves

Interest Rate Modeling and the Risk Premiums in Interest Rate Swaps
Robert Brooks, CFA

Sales-Driven Franchise Value
Martin L. Leibowitz